From Van Valkenburg to Vollick

Vol. 1: The Loyalist Isaac Van Valkenburg aka Vollick and his Vollick & Follick Children

By Lorine McGinnis Schulze

Publisher Olive Tree Genealogy

ISBN: 978-0-9880887-9-5
Cover image 1835 Watercolour by Robert Petley
Credit: Library and Archives Canada, Acc. No. 1938-220-1, C-115424

INTRODUCTION

This book was many years in the making. I first discovered my Van Valkenburg roots in 1993 while attempting to find the parents of my Loyalist ancestor Isaac Vollick. It was then that I discovered Isaac had been born a Van Valkenburg in 1732 in Schoharie, New York. The name change fascinated me, and researching further back in time to the immigrant Van Valkenburg ancestor in America led me to the fascinating and complex story of the Dutch in New Netherland (present day New York state) in the 1620s.

Due to the complexity and sheer volume of my research on Isaac's ancestors and descendants, I made a decision to publish Isaac's story in several volumes. Volume 1 is the story of Isaac and his wife Anna Maria (Mary) after they arrived in Upper Canada (present day Ontario) in 1782. Included are details of Isaac's ancestors back to the first settlement of New Amsterdam (present day New York City) and Albany in the 1620s, Mary's ancestors back to the 1709 Palatine immigration from Germany to New York. Subsequent volumes will discuss each of Isaac and Mary's children, and follow their descendants.

Volume 1 includes various documents, such as Isaac's Land Petitions, Affidavits of witnesses regarding his Loyalty to the British Crown, Letters about Mary and her children and their ordeal in the woods of northern New York in 1779 after American Patriots burned their home and forced the family northward to Canada, and more.

Subsequent volumes on Isaac and Mary's children will also include documents – land petitions, letters, wills, census records, newspaper articles, family photographs and more.

I hope that other descendants will find their stories as fascinating as I do.

Lorine McGinnis Schulze

Table of Contents

Isaac Van Valkenburg aka Vollick

Isaac Van Valkenburg (aka Vollick), born in 1732 in Schoharie, New York, was a United Empire Loyalist who fled the United States and settled in the Niagara area of Upper Canada (present day Ontario) in 1782. He joined Butler's Rangers in 1778 and served until the end of the American Revolution in 1782.

Isaac was the illegitimate son and only child of Isaac Van Valkenburg and Maria Bradt Isaac used his father's surname of Van Valkenburg until 1782. During his years as a private in Butler's Rangers, Isaac's surname changed from Van Valkenburg to Valk or Valck which means 'falcon'. It is my belief that Valk may have been his nickname and on being recorded by English clerks, a vowel was inserted between the final 'l' and 'k' making the surname Valic or Volick. Over the years, the surname was written as Vollick, Volic, Valic, Valck, Valk, Volk and Follick (the German Dutch accent making a 'v' sound like 'f' to English ears).

Isaac was baptised in December 1732 in Schoharie New York as Isaac Falkenburg.[1] Falkenburg is another rendering of the surname Van Valkenburg. Although his father is not listed in the church record of little Isaac's baptism, the sponsors at Isaac's baptism in the High and Low Dutch Church were Isaac and Lydia Falkenburg [sic] his paternal grandparents. Lydia was the daughter of one of the founders of Schenectady New York, the half Dutch and half Mohawk Jacques Cornelise Van Slyke. It is through Isaac the Loyalist that Follick and Vollick descendants claim their Mohawk heritage. Isaac's great-great-grandmother was Ots-Toch a half French, half Mohawk woman who married Cornelis Van Slyke, a Dutchman who settled in Albany New York in 1627.

There is no record of a marriage between Isaac's father Isaac Van Valkenburg and his mother, Maria Bradt. Isaac's name does not appear in the church baptismal records, but the fact that the paternal grandparents were sponsors indicates a level of acceptance at what was most likely an illegitimate birth. We lose track of little Isaac for the next few years after his baptism, and whether he lived with his mother Maria, his father Isaac or his grandparents, is not known.

On 28 May 1737, when Isaac was 5 years old, his father married Jannetje Clement in Albany New York. His father and step-mother moved to Pennsylvania and started a family and there is some thought that little Isaac may have lived with them until the American Revolution. There is no definitive proof of this however.

We hear nothing of Isaac the Loyalist until his marriage to Anna Maria (Mary) Warner, in Schoharie County New York a few days after Christmas 1756. Anna Maria was descended from the Palatine family of Werner, who fled religious persecution in Germany for New York in 1709. As was customary with German families of that time, her middle name of Maria (aka Mary) was the name she was known by, the first name being a formal name not used by the individual.

At some point Isaac and his wife Mary left Schoharie County for northern New York, and settled near the North River.

In the turbulent years of the American Revolution Isaac was arrested three times in New York because of his British sympathies. According to Isaac's land petitions in Upper Canada in 1797, he entered the service of Butler's Rangers in 1778, but on 15 June 1777 his name is found in the Indian Department of Butler's Rangers at half-pay. [2] On *A List of Persons Employed as Rangers in The Indian Department, June 15, 1777*, *Pay New York Currency* we find a list of 67 men paid at 4/per day and then: *"at 2/ per day, [#] 68: Isaac Van Valken Burg "* [3]

Isaac is found on the pay list of Captain William Caldwell's Company of Butler's Rangers 24 December 1777 to 24 October 1778. He is listed as Private Isaac Volkenberg, receiving 2/day. [4] Butler's Rangers was led by Col. John Butler, whose wife Catrina Bradt was Isaac's cousin by virtue of his mother Maria Bradt. Many of the men in Butler's Rangers were related to one another, or to Col. Butler's wife Catrina, and many, like Isaac, had Indian ancestry.

Isaac Volleck [sic] is also found on the pay list of Cpt. John McDonald's Company in Butler's Rangers from 1 May 1778 to 24 October 1777 (Obviously there is an error in dates) Isaac Falk [sic] is found on this same list from 1 May 1778 to 24 October 1778 [5]

During the time that Isaac was fighting with Butler's Rangers, Mary continued to aid the British. In 1779 she and the children were taken from their home at North River, New York, by American patriots. Their home was burned, and Mary and her children were marched 80 miles north through the forest and left in destitute circumstances. The family made their way to Canada and reached Montreal by July 1779. Isaac eventually joined them and the family received food rations, lodging and blankets until 1782 when they settled in the Niagara area as impoverished Loyalists.

Butler's Rangers

Butler's Rangers was the most active and successful regiment in the Northern Department. The men in it ranged over the Kentucky Valley to the boundary of New Jersey, along the frontier of New York and Pennsylvania and westward into the Ohio Valley. Butler's Rangers was the third provincial corps attached to the Northern Department and it had special status due to an arrangement which his commander, John Butler, made with Governor Sir Guy Carleton.

The tactics adopted by Butler were those used with devastating effect during the Seven Years' War by Robert Rogers. Butler and Rogers agreed that the first requirement for a Ranger was that he be able to endure severe hardship for long periods of time, far from any comforts of civilization. Where most regular troops and provincials went into winter quarters, rangers were expected to operate all year round. In summer they marched or travelled by bateaux or canoes; in winter they used sleighs, skates or snowshoes.

Their key to success was their mobility and they travelled with the minimum of equipment. Because there are no war diaries, or records of which specific soldiers were engaged in which battles, we have no way of knowing where Isaac fought or the experiences he endured. We might expect that he was with the Rangers at all times, so wherever Captain Caldwell and Captain McDonald's companies were is likely to be where Isaac saw action.

Loyalists

Many Loyalists and their families were forced to flee America for Canada. On June 26, 1778 190 pounds of Halifax currency was given for expenses incurred by "a number of distressed families of Royalists" who had taken refuge in Quebec "from the Rebellion Provinces"

The Loyalists were part of a forced exile, and, as with all refugees, the sense of dislocation and distress weighed heavily in the migration. What looked, on paper, like an orderly pattern of settlement was in reality a time of confusion and frustration. Individuals and families dissatisfied with their new conditions picked up and moved on. With minimal British aid, they suffered the privation of starting all over, facing late plantings, starvation, and a pristine wilderness.

On 25 July 1779 we find Isaac and his family in Montreal, Quebec. He is with others on a list of *"Loyalists receiving Provisions and not paying for same, in the District of Montreal from 25 July 1779 to 20 August following"*. The family is recorded as one male, one female, one male over 10 and 3 females over 10, receiving 3 1/2 rations daily. On 25 Sept. 1779 they are found in St. Claire, Quebec as impoverished Loyalist Isaac Von Volkenberg [sic]. They are listed as "employed in billets". There were 6 family members total. A total of 120 people were billeted at St. Claire. From Sept 25, 1779 to October 24, 1779 Isaac and his family received 3 1/2 rations daily, at no cost.

In July 1784 a list was taken of *"Persons who have inscribed their names in order to settle and cultivate the Crown Transfer of -- to Niagara"* Included were Isaac Volick [sic] with 1 female, 5 children over 10, 1 child under 10 receiving a total of 7 1/2 rations daily.

By 8 April 1784 Isaac had accepted this opportunity to settle elsewhere, and is found with his family in the brand new settlement on the west side of the River Niagara, Niagara-on-Lake Ontario. An official survey of the new settlement of Niagara lists "Return of Rise and Progress of a Settlement of Loyalists on the West side of the River Niagara, 18 April 1784" and shows Isaac Vollick with 11 acres and a house 18' x 15'. By 14 December 1786 they were living near what is now St. Catharine's, Ontario. They appear on a Victualing List for rations for those Loyalists living in Murray's District, as Isaac and wife with 3 sons over 10 and 2 daughters over 10.

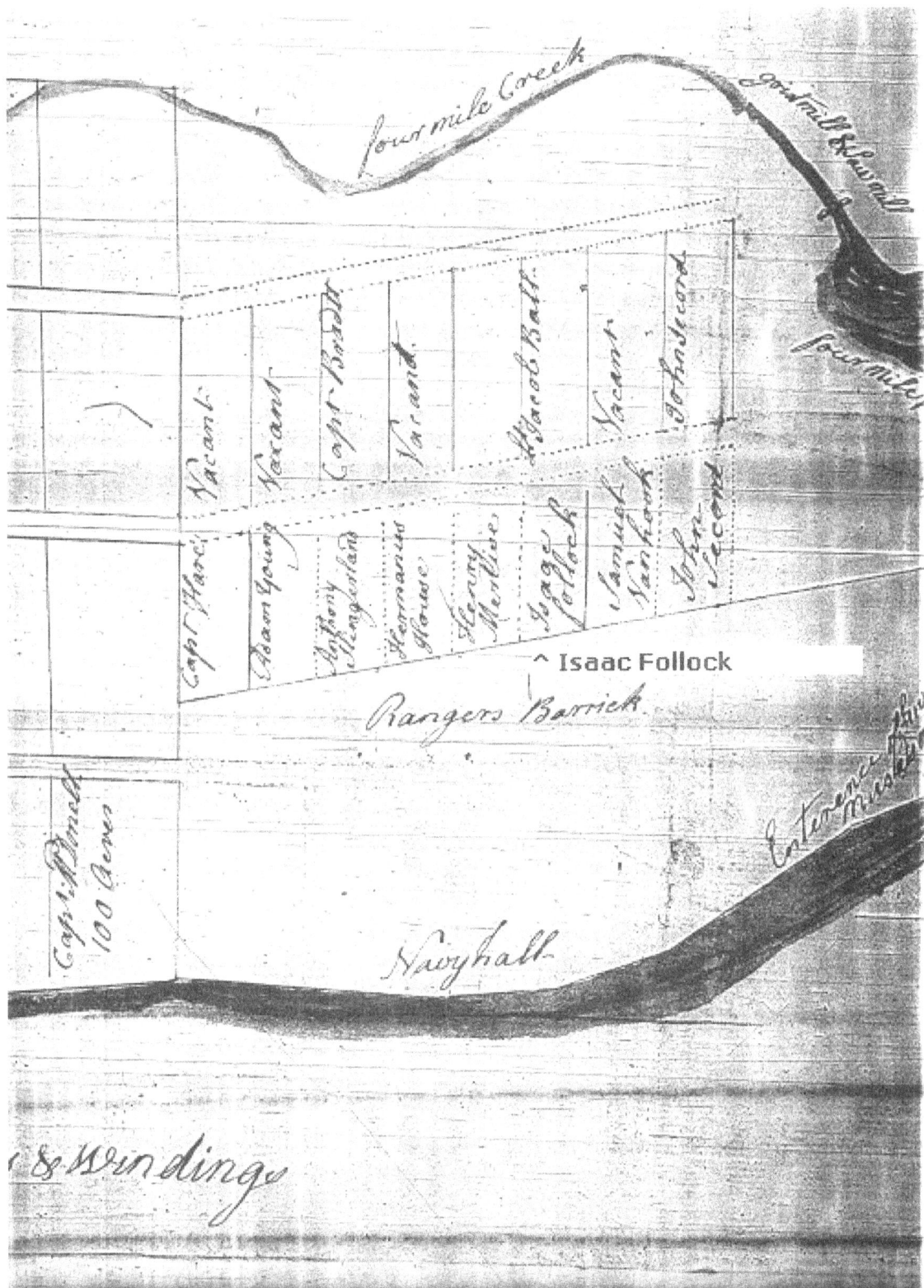

This undated map of the area where Butler's Rangers Barracks was located, shows Isaac Follick's land. Careful scrutiny of the lettering reveals that the first letter of the last name is an "F" rendered as we would now render a lower case letter "f" and not a "P" as many researchers have stated previously. A comparison of the "f" in "four mile" at the top of the map with the first letter of Isaac's surname shows they are identical.

In 1787 Isaac and Mary are found on a list of those who settled near Mills Creek, along with 2 adult sons (not named but almost certainly Mathias and Cornelius) and their son Storm.

The Loyalists did not have an easy time of it. Promises made by the British Government were often broken. In 1788 the Loyalists suffered greatly during what is known as "The Hungry Year". Crops had failed, the winter of 1787 had been brutal and the settlers found themselves with little to eat. Many were forced to share a beef bone from a butchered animal and pass it from house to house to be boiled for whatever nutrition could be gained from it. The bark of certain trees was boiled and eaten.

Isaac and Mary in Niagara

In October 1788 Col. John Butler wrote the following letter in which he mentions Isaac Valk [sic] and other Loyalists who were about to lose the lands he had assured them they could settle on in 1780.

Niagara, 12 Oct. 1788

Sir - In compliance with his Excellency Lord Dorchester Directions communicated through you, dated 17 September last, I shall explain to you, as near as the Papers at present in my Possession will admit of, by what Authority I settled the People on Crown Lands, which now fall with the Garrison Line.

In the month of July 1780, a Memorandum was handed me by His Excellency General Haldimand,setting forth in what manner I was to settle the Loyalists on Crown Lands at Niagara, an order was sent at the same time to Lt. Colonel Bolton (who then commanded at this Fort) to give me such Assistance as was necessary. Upon my arrival at Niagara Lt. Col. Bolton requested the Memorandum to take a copy of it, but never returned it to me, as near as I can recollect the --ports of it were as follows:

//That I should settle such of the Loyalists Families as were already here, upon Crown Lands on the West side of the River at Niagara, also those who should ocme in, or wished to settle, allowing to each Head of a family 200 acres, they were to be furnished with Farming Utensils, feed given, a Blacksmith, & some breeding Cows without any other Consideration, then to give the Garrison the Preference of their Produce at a reasonable Price, or if government took their lands from them, or they chose to leave them,in either case they were to be paid a reasonable Price for their Improvements//

I consulted with the Commanding Officer upon this Business, who agreed with me, that there should be a reserve of lands for the Use of the Crown to extend on the Lake to the One Mile run, & up the River to a place called The Deep Hollow, about two miles from the Point of the Lake, A Survey of which was sent down and approved by His Excellency General Haldimand. I had then orders to discharge each of the Rangers as were old, had families, & give them lands to improve which also allowed others of the Rangers who had Families to improve lands as near the Line as they conveniently could, in order to have the Settlement compact,and the Inhabitants near at hand, I also allowed some of the Officers to improve upon the received Lands, who looked upon their Situation to be temporary, & subject to the Commanding Officer's Pleasure.These people continued unmolested in the Improvements until my departure to England in 1784, but on my return in 1786 I was informed that the received Lands had been extended to the Four Mile Creek, which took in the Improvements made by the undermentioned people, who had been settled by my diretions, & come under the Description set forth in the Memorial,viz:

John Secord, John Secord Jr., Jacob Ball, Anothony Slingerland, Peter Ball, William Pickard, Jacob Van hook, Isaac Valk, John Mattice, Hermanus House

I have enclosed xxx describing the farms, & present lines, with a copy of the directions, the Surrogate received on that subject, but not having the Memorandums in my Possession by which I settled these people, have enclosed extracts from Major Mattheur's Letter on that business, whih, with the Information [?] be able to give, will (I presume to hope) prove satisfactory to his Lordship.

I have the Honor to be Sir, your most obedient and humble servant

John Butler [6]

Copy

Niagara 12th Octr. 1788.

Sir.

In compliance with His Excellency
Lord Dorchesters Directions communicated
through you, dated 17th September last, I shall
explain to you, as near as the Papers at present
in my Possession will admit of, by what Authority
I settled the People on Crown Lands, which now
fall within the Garrison Line.

In the month of July 1780, a Memorandum
was handed me by His Excellency General Hal-
-dimand, setting forth in what manner, I was
to settle the Loyalists on Crown Lands at Niaga-
-ra, an order was sent at the same time to Lt.
Colonel Bolton (who then commanded at this
Port) to give me such Assistance as was necessary.
Upon my Arrival at Niagara Lt. Col. Bolton
requested the Memorandum to take a Copy
of it, but never returned it to me, As near as I
can recollect the Purports of it were as follow,
"that I should settle such of the Loyalists Fami-
"-lies as were already here, upon Crown Lands on
"the West side of the River at Niagara, also those who
"should come in, & wished to settle; allowing to
"each Head of a Family 200 Acres, they were to be

JBL.

Lt. Col: Hunter.

"furnished with Farming Utensils, Seed Grain, a
Blacksmith, & some breeding Cows without any other
Consideration; than to give the Garrison the Refuse
of their Produce at a reasonable Price, & if Government
took their Lands from them, or they chose
to leave them, in either case they were to be paid
a reasonable Price for their Improvements."

    I consulted with the Commanding Officer
upon this Business, who agreed with me, that there
should be a reserve of Lands for the Use of the Crown
to extend on the Lake to the one Mile run, & up
the River to a place called the deep Hollow, about
two miles from the Point of the Lake, a survey of
which was sent down, & approved by His Excellency General Haldimand, I had then Orders to
discharge such of the Rangers as were old, & had
Families, & give them Lands to improve which
& also allowed others of the Rangers who had Families
to improve Lands as near the Line, as they conveniently could; in order to have the Settlement
compact, and the Inhabitants near at hand, I
also allowed some of the Officers to improve upon
the reserved Lands, who looked upon their Situation to be temporary, & subject to the Commanding Officers Pleasure. —— These People continued unmolested in their Improvements
till my departure for England in 1784, but on
my Return in 1786. I was informed that the
reserved Lands, had been extended to the

18

four Mile Creek, which took in the Improve
:ments made by the undermentioned People, who
had been settled by my Directions, & come under
the Description set forth in the Memorial viz:
John Secord, John Secord junr. Jacob Ball, An=
thony Slingerland, Peter Ball, William Pickard,
Jacob: Vanhook, Isaac Vath, John Mattice,
Hermanus, House.

I have enclosed a survey describing both
the former, & present Lines, with a Copy of the Direc:
:tions, the Surveyor received on that Subject, but
not having the Memorandums in my Possession
by which I settled these People; have enclosed
Extracts from Major. Matthews Letter, on that
Business, which with the Information he was
be able to give, will (I presume to hope) prove
satisfactory to His Lordship,

I have the Honor to be
Sir
Your most obedient, & most
Humble Servant

(Signed) John, Butler.

The story of Isaac and his children can be found in the early land records and petitions of Upper Canada over the next 20 years. There are few records available for these early years of settlement in what is now the Province of Ontario, and we must be content with what the land records and other miscellaneous records reveal.

Many Loyalists were farmers and land was the key to survival. Lands were allotted to settlers according to rank and status. The head of a family received 100 acres, each additional family member adding on 50 acres. A single man was entitled to 50 acres, a private in the Provincial Corps to 100 acres, and non-commissioned officers received 200 acres. An additional 200 acres were granted to heads of families who had improved their land by 1787. In 1788 all grants to officers were raised to the level of those granted to the 84th Regiment (Royal Highland Emigrants) so that field officers received 5,000 acres, with 3,000 for captains and 2,000 for subalterns. Land boards were created to administer the growing complexity of property and Loyalist privileges.

Land was at the root of constitutional agitation in the new settlement. Under the provisions of the Quebec Act of 1774 and the royal instructions of July 16, 1783, Loyalists received their lands as tenants, with the king as their feudal seigneur. Loyalists sought a number of changes; those included English laws, town meetings, lands held in free and common usage and a transfer of authority from military to civil control. Their lobbying led to the Constitutional Act of 1791 which split the old Province of Quebec and created Lower and Upper Canada.

In June of 1792 the new Lieutenant Governor, the former commander of the Loyalist Queen's Rangers during the American Revolution, Colonel John Graves Simcoe, set out for Upper Canada. In 1794 the major posts at Niagara and Detroit remained key centres of inland trade and British military security. At Niagara on the Upper Canadian side of the river an early town was forming, which Simcoe called Newark, later Niagara-on-the-Lake. Simcoe temporarily made Newark his seat of government. There on September 17, 1792 he met the province's first legislature in newly built Freemasons' Hall. This small parliament passed into effect English civil law and trial by jury, re-titled the four existing districts of Upper Canada from Luneburg, Mecklenburg, Nassau and Hesse to Eastern, Midland, Home and Western, provided a court house and jail in each, and set up other basic administrative machinery.

In 1795, Isaac Vollick petitioned for, and received, a free grant of land Concession 6 Lots 6 (200 acres), 7 (200 acres), N. half Lot 8 (100 acres) in East Flamborough Township, Wentworth County, on 10 March 1797 being granted 500 acres total for his family lands. It is doubtful that Isaac ever lived on the land in Flamborough, although evidence exists that at least two of his sons did. Of interest is the fact that Isaac's son Cornelius (recorded as "Fallock"), was also granted land (200 acres) in East Flamborough on 10 March 1797 - he received land bordering his father's - Concession 5, Lot 7. On the same date, Jonas Larroway, father-in-law to Cornelius Vollick, was granted 200 acres of land on Concession 10, Lot 3.

Isaac's son Storm received land in West Flamborough Township, on 10 August 1801, being 100 acres on Concession 5, the south half of Lot 7. Land ownership is one of the ways we can determine where Isaac's grandchildren fit, that is, which son of Isaac's is their father.

Concession 6, Lot 6 was Crown Land before being granted to Isaac, and the next transaction on this land is from William Dickson to Isaac Todd on 10 June 1802. [7] Concession 6, Lot 7 was also Crown Land before Isaac received it and the next transaction on it was on 18 June 1802 when William Dickson sold it to Isaac Todd. At some point it was in the hands of his son Storm because on 5 Feb 1838 Storm is recorded as selling the east half to James Hainer.

A certificate of Robert Kerr, JP dated 17 October 1795 states that Adrian and Christian Bradt, living at 12-Mile Creek, are married to the daughters of Isaac Follick [sic], a reduced soldier in Butler's Rangers. [8] Isaac himself petitioned that same day to have William Dickson locate his granted 500 acres of land on his behalf.

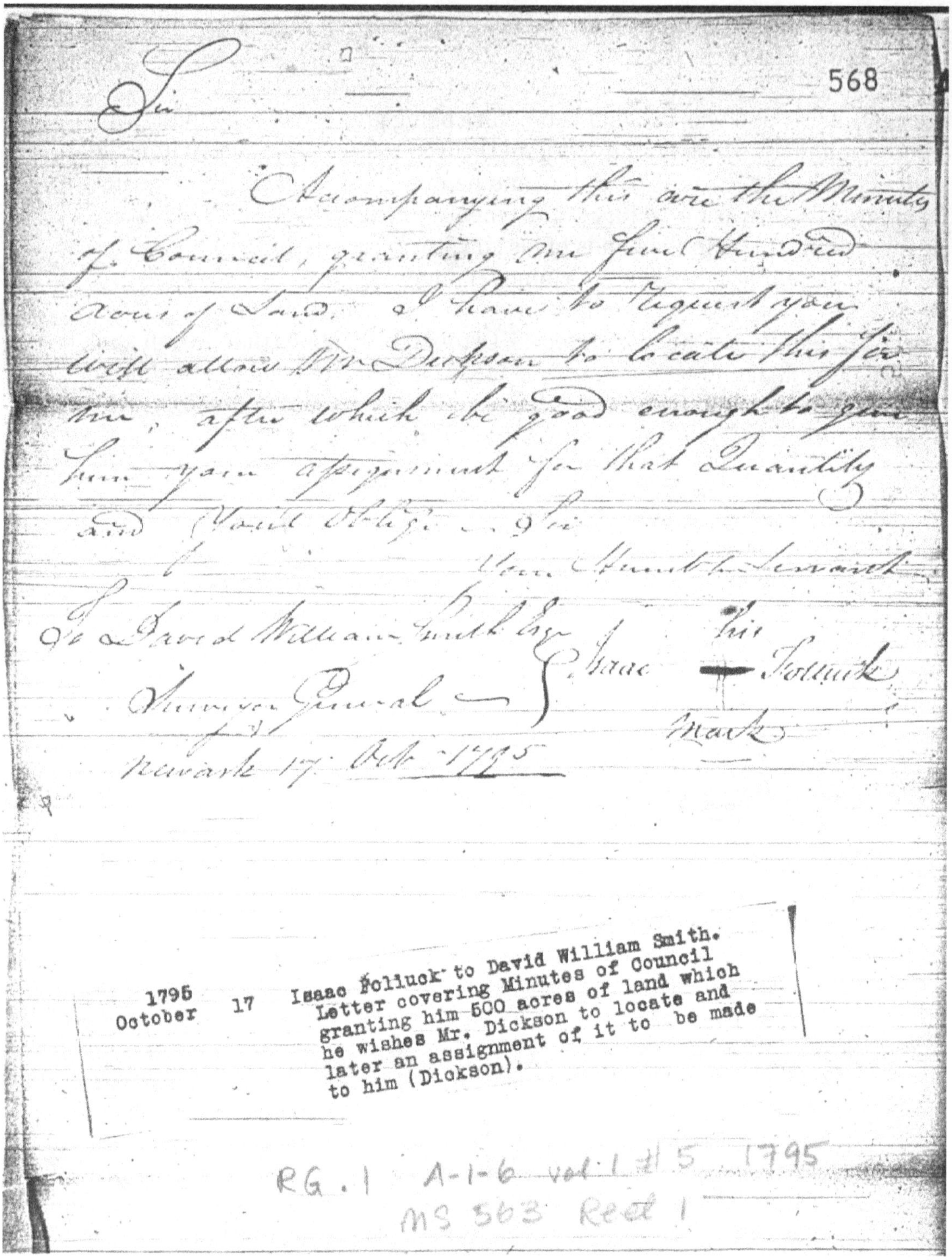

568

Sir

Accompanying this are the Minutes of Council, granting me five hundred acres of Land. I have to request you will allow Mr Dickson to locate this for me, after which be good enough to give him your assignment for that Quantity and Your Oblig... Sir

Your Humble Servant

To David William Smith Esqr Surveyor General

Isaac his Folluck mark

Newark 17 Oct 1795

1795 October 17 Isaac Folluck to David William Smith. Letter covering Minutes of Council granting him 500 acres of land which he wishes Mr. Dickson to locate and later an assignment of it to be made to him (Dickson).

RG. 1 A-1-6 vol 1 #5 1795
MS 563 Reel 1

Sir – Accompanying this are the Minutes of Council, granting me five hundred acres of Land. I have to request you will allow Mr. Dickson to locate this for me after which be good enough to give him your assignment for that quantity and Your oblig... your Humble Servant, Isaac Folluck (his mark). To David William Smith Esq, Surveyor General. Newark 17 Oct. 1795

On 17 March 1797 Isaac received another free grant of 300 acres of land on Concession 3, Lots 1 & 3, Louth Twp. Lincoln Co. (between Port Dalhousie and St. Catharine's) as military lands. On 4 April 1797 he received a free grant of land for Concession 4, Lots 22 & 23 Grantham Twp. Lincoln Co. This land in Louth and Grantham Twp. touches - it is coincidence that the township boundaries run through its centre. The land he received is approximately 2 miles north of present-day Pt. Dalhousie and 1 mile south east of St. Catherines. This land is where he actually settled, and built his home.

To His Honor Peter Russell Esqr administering
the Government of the Province of Upper Canada
in Council —

      The Petition of Isaac Pollock —

Humbly Sheweth.

    That your Petitioner served in
Col. Butlers Rangers, has been Since the
Reduction of said Corps settled on his Lands
but as that has received no Authority
sufficient for the Surveyor General to assign
the same, Prays your Honor to Confirm him
in his right to three hundred acres, as a
Reduced soldier, and as his wife the Mother
of a large family, has never in her
right drawn any Lands Prays your Honor
will Grant Her whatever Quantity you
in Your Wisdom May think proper and
She in Duty bound Your Petitioner will
ever Pray & Likewise, asks to be allowed to locate
a Lot in the Town of Newark —

            Isaac Pollock

Recd 16th March 1797 —

To his Honour Peter Russell Esq., administering the Government of the Province of Upper Canada in Council. The petition of Isaac Folluck, Humbly Sheweth, that your petitioner served in Col. Butler's Rangers, has been during the Reduction of the said Corps, settled on his lands but as -- --- --- no authority sufficient for the Surveyer General to assign -- -- prays your Honor to confirm in his right to 300 acres as a reduced soldier, and as his wife, the mother of a large family, has never in her right drawn any lands, prays your Honor will grant her whatever quantity you in your wisdom may think proper, and as in Duty Bound, your Petitioner will Ever Pray --, prays to be allowed to locate a lot in the Town of Newark. Isaac Folluck. 16 March 1797

Isaac Follack

16 March '97.

Read march 17th '97.

Recommended 300 acres as military lands.

Confirmed P.R.

Gave a warrant ---

Entered Page 255

A 2 page document conferred on Isaac Vollock [sic] of the Township of Louth in the County of Lincoln, in the District of Niagara, Yeoman, Lot numbers one and three in the Third Concession of the Township of Louth in the County of Lincoln in the said District of Niagara, a U.E. [9]This land in Louth was eventually disputed and many petitions and documents can be found concerning the dispute.

At the end of March, 1797, Isaac petitioned for land again - this time stating he was a Loyalist, had served in Butler's Rangers since 1778, and had previously received his military lands and 500 acres of family lands for his 10 children, but that he neglected to mention his wife in his earlier petitions. An affidavit from J. Ball stated that Isaac's wife had come to the settlement (Niagara) in 1782.

30 March 1797. I do hereby certify that Isaac Volck served in Butlers Rangers from the year 1778 to the end of the War. That his Wife and family suffered much during his absence. – were sent prisoners a considerable distance from home. J Ball, JP. Newark March 30th 1797. Isaac Volck's wife came to Niagara in the year 1782.

Isaac Volk

27. No. 29

Read 31 March 1797

Ordered 50 acres to make up Petitioners family lands if it shall appear that he received that quantity there of what he was entitled to.

P. R.

Entered

Entered in Land Book B page 28

The Bearer Isaac Folik served with his two sons in Butlers late Corps of Rangers, and came in with his family consisting of Eight Children excluding his two sons who were in the Province in the Spring of 1782. Newark 17 August 1795. Signed R. Clench Lieut. Butlers Late Rangers. Cornelius Folik is married to the daughter of Jonas Larroway an old Ranger, served during the late war. R. Clench.

To his Excellency John Graves Simcoe, Esq.. Lieut. Gov. Upper Canada Major Genl.
Commmanding the Forces in said Province. In Council. The Petition of Isaac Volik Humbly
Sheweth, that your Petitioner served as a Private Soldier in Butlers late Rangers, that your
Petitioner has located his three hundred acres of land, and your Petitioner brought into this
Settlement Eight Children, exclusive of Two Sons who were in the Service, Your Petitioner
therefore humbly Prays that your Excellency will take his ---- into Consideration and be pleased
to allow him some land, in consequence of his having supported so large a Family, and your
Petitioner will as in duty born, Ever Pray – Isaac Folik

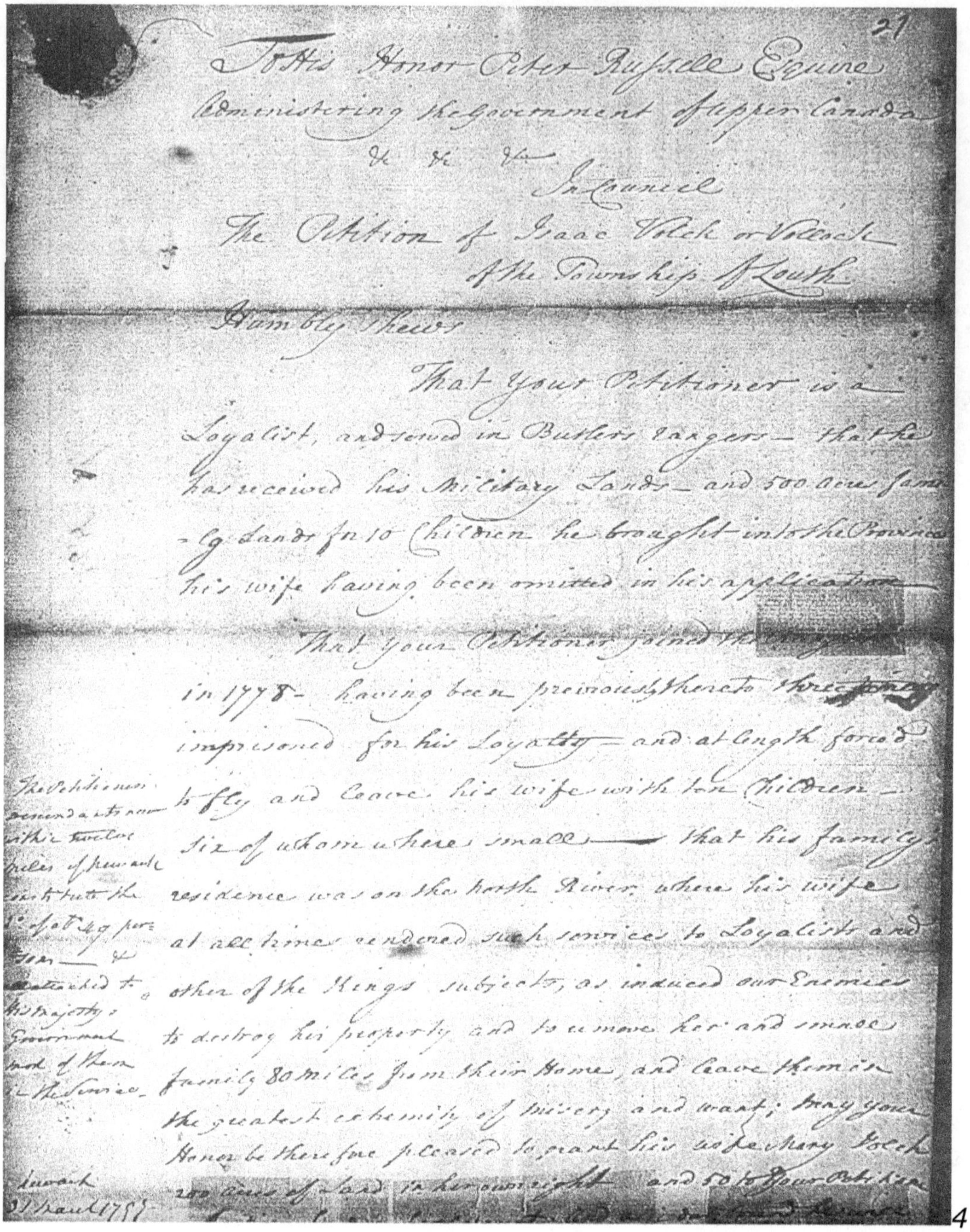
To His Honor Peter Russell Esquire
Administering the Government of Upper Canada
&c &c &c
In Council
The Petition of Isaac Volck or Volleck
of the Township of Louth
Humbly Shews
That your Petitioner is a Loyalist, and served in Butlers Rangers — that he has received his Military Lands — and 500 Acres family Lands for 10 Children he brought into the Province his wife having been omitted in his application
That your Petitioner joined the [illegible] in 1778 — having been previously thereto three times imprisoned for his Loyalty — and at length forced to fly and leave his wife with ten Children — six of whom where small — that his family residence was on the North River, where his wife at all times rendered such services to Loyalists and other of the Kings subjects, as induced our Enemies to destroy his property and to remove her and small family 80 miles from their Home, and leave them in the greatest extremity of misery and want; May your Honor be therefore pleased to grant his wife Mary Volck 200 Acres of Land in her own right and 50 to your Petitioner [illegible]

4

April 1797. In Council 4 April 1797. Granted Isaac Vollock of the Township of Louth in the County of Lincoln, in the District of Niagara, Yeoman. Lot Number 1 and 3 in the First Concession of the Township of Louth in the County of Lincoln in the said District of Niagara, a U. E.

In August 1797 Isaac and his friend Jonas Larroway (who was also the father-in-law to Isaac's son Cornelius Vollick) went to court in a dispute with Peter TenBrock over the land in Louth Township. The documents are dated 28 August 1797 and the final orders were:

- The deed for Lot No. 1 in Concession 3 Louth Township to be issued to Isaac Vollock [sic]
- The deed for Lot No. 2 in Concession 3 Louth Township to be issued to Jonas Laraway
- The deed for Lot No. 22 in Grantham Township, for that portion of the land that lay north of the creek to be issued to TenBrock
- The deed for the rest of Lot No. 22 in Grantham Township to be issued to Isaac Vollock
- The deed for the Lot No. 23 in Concession 3 Grantham Township to be issued to Isaac Vollock after he paid Tenbrock 5 pounds York money per acre for all the improved portion of the lot

In Council Aug.t 28. 1797

Present

His Honor Peter Russell Esq.r
President

The Hon.ble The Chief Justice

The Hon.ble The Speaker

Caveat

Tenbrook — against — Polloch.

d.o — — Lawrence

Ordered

That the Deed for N.o 1
in the 3.d Concession of Louth issue to Polloch

That the Deed for N.o 2
in the same Concession issue to Lawrence

That a Deed for so much
in Grantham
of N.o 22, as lies to the Northward of the
Creek issue to Tenbrook. by consent

That a Deed for the
rest of that lot issue to Polloch

In Council 28 August 1797. Present
His Honor Peter Russel Esq. President.
The Honorable the Chief Justice.
The Honorable The Speaker

Caveat
Tenbrock against Vollock

Tenbrock against Larroway

Ordered that the deed for No. 1 in the 3ʳᵈ Concession of Louth issue to Vollock. That the deed for No. 2 in the same Concession issue to Larroway. That a deed for so much of No. 22 in Grantham as lies to the Northward of the Creek issue to Tenbrock. By consent. That a deed for the rest of that lot issue to Vollock.

That the deed for No. 23, 3ʳᵈ Concession of Grantham, issued to Vollock, he paying to Tenbrock 5pounds York money and so much of the lot as Tenbrock has improved.

Order in Council 29 August 1797
Tenbrock against Vollock
Tenbrock against Larroway

The documents leading up to the dispute were recorded on 17 March 1797. After living on the land in question for twelve years, Isaac and Jonas discovered that Peter TenBrock's name appeared on official records of the land. They petitioned, stating that they fought in the 'late War' (the American Revolution) with Col. Butler, and that they settled nearby in 1784. They took possession of their lands on 12-mile Creek, and had ever since held them by right of occupancy. Since a "spurious claim" had been made against their land, the Land Board refused to grant them their deeds. They continued to live on the land, but now are fighting Peter TenBrock's claim that the land is his. They provided further details, stating that in 1784 Isaac Folluck [sic] settled and took up lots 21 & 22 (note here that Isaac erred, it should have read lots 22 & 23) in Concession 4, Grantham Township, also Lots 1 & 3 on Concession 3, Louth Township. Isaac added that on Lot 21 (should be 22) he raised crops, built a house and barn and then sold that for 100 pounds to John Gould. Isaac then built another house and barn on Lot 1 & 3 of Louth, and still lives there on more than 20 acres of cleared land.

There has been an error by the surveyor, and Nicholas Smith's name has been inserted on the map where Isaac's name should appear, but Nicholas is prepared to swear that he has no claim to the land. Peter TenBrock however, whose name also appears in error on the Grantham land, is threatening to drive Isaac and Jonas out from their homes and take possession of the land. Isaac tells the court that he agreed to give TenBrock half of Lot 21 (should read 22) but the other half has been improved, and sold by Isaac to John Gould, who is now threatening Isaac with prosecution for false sale if he (john) does not get good title to the land he purchased.

Isaac and Jonas point out that TenBrock has already received 1,400 acres and they wish to convince the court of the justice of their claim, and the injustice of TenBrock trying to deprive *"in their old age two men who with the descendants now within twelve miles of Newark, constitute the number of 60 - Isaac Folluck 49 and Jonas Laroway 11, and all of age in His Majesty's Service"*

Isaac asks to be confirmed in half of Lot 21 (should read 22) of Grantham and Lots 1 & 3 in Louith, while Jacob asks for confirmation of his land in Lot 2 in Louth. Affidavits with these petitions state that Isaac Volluck served in Butler's Rangers and brought his family into the Province (now Ontario) in 1782, that he also had two sons who served in Butler's Rangers. The Surveyor General's report was given on 4 April 1797, stating that Vollick and Laroway had been in possession of the lands for 12 years, Vollick on Lots 22 & 23, Concession 4 Grantham Township as well as Lots 1 & 3, Concession 3 Louth, with Laraway on Lot 2 of Concession 3 Louth. It was ordered by the court that the Petitioners be confirmed in their lands, including all improvements made. Warrants were given to both men on 5 April 1797.

A further complication to the case was that Nicholas Smith was found to have the assignment of Lot 21, Concession 4, Grantham Township, while Isaac Vollick had Lots 22 & 23. All these lots were claimed by Peter Tenbrock, also for Lot 3, Concession 3 of Louth. Tenbrock claims to have been assigned the land in Louth and that Lots 1 & 2 also had his name entered on them. TenBrock petitioned to be given Lots 22 & 23 in Grantham in place of Lot 30, Concession 5 and Lot 30 Concession 4 of Ancaster, which he claims to have received in error. TenBrock stated that an old plan had the names of Isaac Volluck and NIcholas Smith on the Grantham land but that these claims were never authenticated. Tenbrock also petitioned for Lots 1 & 2 on Concession 4 of Louth Township which had been assigned to Richard Hainer (who was married to one of Isaac Vollick's daughters)

Further notes are given in the court's consideration of the case - that the land where Nicholas Smith's name is entered in error (and for which Isaac Vollick claimed half), Tenbrock has promised that when he receives the Certificate for Lot 22, Concession 4, Grantham, that he will allow Nicholas to keep all the land he has improved on that lot, as long as Smith gives him (TenBrock) an equal quantity of woodland on the North end of Lots 20 & 21.

In November 1798 Peter TenBroek wrote a letter about the land dispute.

12 Mile Creek Nov. 29, 1798

Gentlemen

Have been informed a few days ago that a Land Board was to vote on the 30th Instant and that one isaac Volck whome I am in dispute with, concerning wo lots of land, which he claims from me, and has sold, where he has no right to, under any pretence whatsoever, according to Justice ----, as also according to the First Regulations of that Board made, and am the oldest proprietor of the said lands, and by Order of the Commanding Officer then here, was survey to me by the Engineer and can prove my prior right to the said lands, therefore hope that the Board will not proceed to give him tickets for the said land and lots in dispute as will appear on the map thereof. Am not well enough to attend the Board at the day, but any other day, when the Board meets again will attend on notice with my Evidence, in order to prove my prior right to said lots of land.

12 mile Creek Nov.r 29 1793

Gentlemen
172

Have been Inform.d a few days
ago, that a Land Board was to sit on the
30.th Instant, and that one Israel Polck whom
I am in Dispute with, Concerning two Lotts
of Land, which he Claims from me, and
has sold, where he has no Right to, under
any pretence whatsomever, According to
Justice & Equity of Law, as also, According
to the first Regulations of that Board
made, and am the Oldest proprietar
of the said Lands, and by order of
the Commanding Officer, then here,

was Survey'd to me, By the Engineer,
and Can prove my prior Right
to the Said lands, therefore hope that
the Board will Not proceed to give
him Tickets for the Said lands In Dispute
                                    or Lotts
as will appear on the map thereof
am Not well Enough to attend the
Board at that Day, But any Other
Day, when the Board meets again,
will attend on Notice, with my
Evidences in Order to prove my
prior Right to said Lotts of land—

    Gentlemen
    I Remain your Very
Humbl Serv——
Peter Ten Broeck

A record was made 21 April 1803 in the Upper Canada Land Board Records and
Minutes regarding the lands of Isaac Vollick and Jonas Larroway. [11]

In 1804 Isaac and Tenbrock were in court again. They appeared before the Executive Council to dispute land. On 17 March 1804 we find court documents over disputed land claim Concession 3, Lot 3 Louth Twp. Lincoln Co. and on 7 April 1804 over the disputed land claim on Concession 3, Lot 1 Louth Twp. [12] They include a note that Captain Peter Tenbrook received Lot 1 on Concession 3 in Louth Township but the deed was never completed. A copy of Isaac's Land Grant and his OC (Order in Council) for the same land is also presented. The grant describes the land and states that it is 100 acres. Isaac's Certificate for Land is also in this bundle as well as a letter from Mr. Hamilton of Queenston, dated March 1803 and asking "..if Isaac Volluck is not on the same plan [the Quebec Plan] on Lot No. 1 in the 3rd Concession of Louth" and "the reason, if known, why the deed for Vollock's land, has not --." Hamilton goes on to state that he wishes to Mortgage the lot but without the deed, he can only do before the Commissioner.

Following are the documents from 1804 including the copy of Isaac's Order in Council from 1797. This is the last record we have of Isaac the Loyalist.

0120

Mr Small the farmer
St James's reque 1804

Isaac Vollenks

Capt Petro Seabrook

Ent Book Lett recd
No 14 p 1743
JH

0121

Council Office
7 April 1804

Sir

Mr. Jarvis informs
that there has not been a Deed
completed to late Peter Timbrook
for Lot No. 1. in the 3d Con. of Louth

I am Sir
(Sig) A. Granville
Secretary
J. Small
C. Ex.

The Sur Genl
Surveyor

33

GRANT to *Isaac Vollock*,

of the Townſhip of *Louth*

In the County of *Lincoln*,

In the　　　　　Diſtrict *of Niagara, Yeoman his*

all that parcel of Land

In the Townſhip of *Louth*,

In the County of *Lincoln*,

In the　　　　　Diſtrict *of Niagara*　　　　being

Lot Number *1*

In the　　　　　　　　*3* Conceſſion　　　That is to ſa;

commencing in front of the ſaid　　　　　Conceſſion

At the North-Eaſt Angle of　　　　　*the ſaid Lot in the Center*

Boundary line of the Township

Then South　　Degrees　　Minutes Eaſt　*20* Chains　*Jan*

ſame or leſs, to the ſtream as paſſed in center of the

township

Then South　Degrees　　Minutes Weſt　*20* Chains

more or leſs, to the limit between lot No 1 & 2

Then North　Degrees　　Minutes Weſt　*50* Chains

more or leſs, to the ſtream as paſſed in center of the

Then North　　Degrees　　Minutes Eaſt　*20* Chains

more or leſs

To the place of beginning

containing　*200*　　Acres　　　more or leſs

OIC 4 Apr. 1797　Grant dated 7 Apr. 1804

34

No. 1 Grant, J. 3d

Isaac Pollock ...

South District L. Niagara

... in the ... office

1804

...

... H.G. Govr. **PROVINCE OF UPPER** ...

GEORGE THE THIRD, by the Grace of God of the United Kingdom of ...
the Faith :....... To all to whom these Presents sh...

KNOW YE, that We of Our special grace, certain knowledge, and mere motion have Given and Gra...

... heirs and assigns for ever: All that parcel or tract of Land situate ...

in our said Province, containing by admeasurement ...

together with all the woods and waters thereon lying, and being under the reservations, limitations, and conditions hereinafter expressed ... and bounded, or may be otherwise known as follows: that is to say ...

... twenty ...

Fifty Chains more or less ... allowance ...

Plan of beginning

Portion of Certificate for Land L.1.C. 3 South Twp. Lincoln Co. to Isaac Pollock

TO HAVE AND TO HOLD ...

Gentlemen

Will you have the goodness to ascertain whether the Name William Stevens is not on the Quebec Plan on land in the Gore of the Township of Stamford & Niagara near where those Townships corner on Grantham & Thorold.

Also if Isaac Pollucks is not on the same plan on Lott No. 1 in the 3 Concession of Louth. If these names are found on the Plan I will be further thankfull to ask for a Certificate to this purpose That you

you mention the reason (if known) why the deed of for Pollucks land at least, has not issued. I wish to ascertain Mortgages on both these Lotts, which for want of the Deed can only be done before the Commissioner This I trust will plead my excuse for this trouble — give one

I am Gentlemen
your very hum Sert
C. Hamilton

To Theirs & Lieut

Queenston March 4. 1818

In Council 4th April 1794

Granted Isaac Pollock of the Township of
Louth, in the County of Lincoln, in the
District of Niagara, Yeoman. Lots numbered
one, and three in the Twelve Concession, of
the Township of Louth, in the County of
Lincoln in the said District of Niagara
a U. E. —————————

                                    Wm Jarvis
                                      & c.

Secretary General

... Pollock of Leith, our ... ... with Col ... ... before the Executive ... for ... matter there in the 3rd ... of Leith. This was determined in favour of ... Pollock. ... you the ... ... of a Description ... ... you Office in his name, if not what ... if any reason why .. Your attention ... will oblige ... Your humble Servt

... 17th March ... 1804

To

Anna Maria (Mary) Warner, wife of Isaac the Loyalist

Mary Warner was baptised in the Schoharie Reformed Dutch Church on 22 October 1735 to Johann Matthias (Matthias) Warner and Anna Bellinger. The sponsors were John Fridrich Bauch and his wife Anna Magdalena.

On 28 October 1757 her marriage to Isaac Van Valkenburg was recorded in the Schoharie Lutheran Church, with Isaac's name rendered as "Isaac Falck".

Isaac and Mary's first child Marietie, was baptised 28 May 1758 in Albany [13], followed by Matthias Valck baptised 17 June 1759 in Schoharie [14], Cornelis Vollick baptised 16 Aug 1761 [15] in Albany, Annaje Vollick baptised 26 Jun 1763 in Schoharie [16], Storm Follick baptised 17 Feb 1765 in Schoharie [17], Sophia Vollick baptised 11 Apr 1766 in Schoharie [18], Elizabeth Vollick baptised December 1767 in Schoharie [19], Catharina Vollick baptised 25 June 1769 in Schoharie [20], Sarah Vollick born about 1770 somewhere in New York, John Vollick baptised 25 July 1772 in Berne, and possibly Maria Vollick born sometime in 1775.

Mary's husband Isaac was imprisoned three times by the Americans for his loyalty to the British King. After Isaac joined Butler's Rangers and fled to Canada, Mary was left with ten children, and according to Mary's own testimony, six of them were small. If we look at the birth years of the children, we can see that by 1779 her children were ages 4 to 21, with the six youngest being Maria, John, Sarah, Catharina, Elizabeth, and Sophia who ranged in age from 4 to 13.

Mary continued to aid the British, and in 1779 she and the children were taken from their home at North River, New York, by American patriots. Their home was burned, Mary and the children were marched 80 miles north through the forest and then abandoned there in destitute circumstances. Mary and ten of her children made their way through deep forest to Canada and reached Montreal by July 1779.

They received food rations, lodging and blankets until 1782 when they settled in the Niagara area as impoverished Loyalists.

The Ancestors of the Loyalist Isaac Van Valkenburg aka Vollick

Isaac's ancestors were among the first Dutch settlers to the colony of New Netherland in the early 1600s. They also included French Huguenot and Belgium Walloons who fled religious persecution to settle Harlem New York in the mid 1600s. It was an exciting and tumultuous time for those who dared to embark on the journey from the Netherlands, France and Belgium to a new world.

Isaac's immigrant Van Valkenburg ancestor was Lambert Van Valkenburg who, with his wife, arrived in New Netherland (present day New York) around January 1644 or slightly earlier.

Primary source records from the Netherlands indicate that Lambert's father was most probably Lambert Drieskens Van Valkenburg. [21] Thus the immigrant Lambert's name would be "Lambert Lambertse Van Valkenburg".

The parents of Lambert Drieskens (Andriessen) van Valckenburch who died in Millen 9 March 1651 were Andries van Valckenburch born circa 1540, tailor of Millen. Andries and his wife were both dead by 27 October 1609. In 1595 Lambert Drieskens married Maria and she died 20 October 1650. They were parents of Lambert van Valckenburch baptised at Millen 16 April 1614 and betrothed in Amsterdam 4 January 1642 to Annetje Jacobs (meaning Annetje daughter of Jacob) from Tonningen in Schleswig-Holstein age 20. [22]

The Van Valkenburg Family

Isaac the Loyalist's Van Valkenburg Ancestry

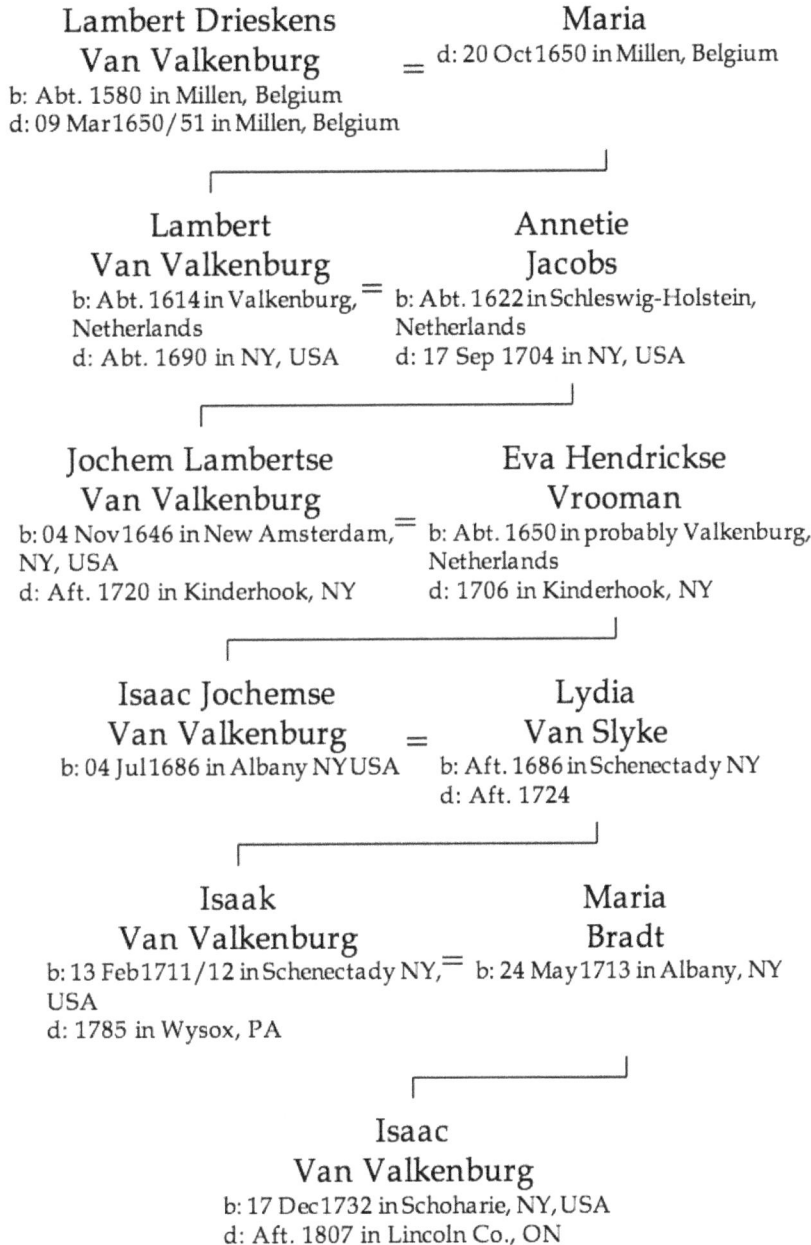

Lambert Drieskens Van Valkenburg
b: Abt. 1580 in Millen, Belgium
d: 09 Mar 1650/51 in Millen, Belgium
=
Maria
d: 20 Oct 1650 in Millen, Belgium

Lambert Van Valkenburg
b: Abt. 1614 in Valkenburg, Netherlands
d: Abt. 1690 in NY, USA
=
Annetie Jacobs
b: Abt. 1622 in Schleswig-Holstein, Netherlands
d: 17 Sep 1704 in NY, USA

Jochem Lambertse Van Valkenburg
b: 04 Nov 1646 in New Amsterdam, NY, USA
d: Aft. 1720 in Kinderhook, NY
=
Eva Hendrickse Vrooman
b: Abt. 1650 in probably Valkenburg, Netherlands
d: 1706 in Kinderhook, NY

Isaac Jochemse Van Valkenburg
b: 04 Jul 1686 in Albany NY USA
=
Lydia Van Slyke
b: Aft. 1686 in Schenectady NY
d: Aft. 1724

Isaak Van Valkenburg
b: 13 Feb 1711/12 in Schenectady NY, USA
d: 1785 in Wysox, PA
=
Maria Bradt
b: 24 May 1713 in Albany, NY

Isaac Van Valkenburg
b: 17 Dec 1732 in Schoharie, NY, USA
d: Aft. 1807 in Lincoln Co., ON

Lambert, the son of Lambert, is not found in any documents in the New World with a patronymic [23]. The patronymic of Jochemse was attached by the National Association of the Van Valkenburg Family based solely on the naming of his first known son as "Jochem". This new evidence indicates that this is an error and that Lambert was not Lambert Jochemse, but Lambert Drieskens.

No record of Lambert and Annetje's arrival by ship in the New World has been found but records found for Lambert Van Valkenburg indicate he was in New Amsterdam as early as January 1644. Since he was married in Amsterdam January 1642 we can narrow his immigration to that two year period (January 1642-January 1644).

From January to June 1644 Lambert was one of the soldiers engaged to fight the Manhattan Indian War. July 1644 saw Lambert purchasing land and a house near Fort Amsterdam (present day New York City)

Lambert and Annetje Van Valkenburg's son Jochem Lambertse Van Valkenburg was baptised in the Reformed Dutch Church of New Amsterdam (present day New York City) on 4 November 1646. [24] Shortly afterwards, Lambert and his growing family moved to another house near Fort Amsterdam.

There are no records found for Lambert from 1647 to 1657, but in 1657 he claimed that two men assaulted him and his wife in their own home and beat them severely. The men he charged claimed that it was Lambert who chased them out of his house with a sword.

At some point before 1657 Lambert became a burgher, meaning he had certain rights and privileges as a citizen of New Amsterdam. Lambert van Valkenborch [sic] is recorded as sergeant of the burgher guard in January 1657. The burgher guard were responsible for walking the streets of the town, checking for fires, suspicious activity, burglary and other crimes, also calling out the hour on every hour. In essence the burgher guard were policemen, firemen and town criers.

Between 1653 and 1658 Lambert had purchased a house nearer Fort Albany (just outside the present day city of Albany) Lambert van Valckenborgh was appointed for the Rattle Watch of Beverwyck (present day Albany) in July 1659. The Rattle Watch consisted of men in the burgher guard.

In May 1660, Lambert joined others in signing a petition requesting that the Dutch be allowed to trade directly with the Indians for fur, instead of going through the West India Company brokers as middlemen. Since it was in the interest of financial gain for the WIC to continue as middlemen, this was not well received, but Lambert and others declared they would trade directly anyway, so the courts reluctantly granted permission. This caused problems, as the Indians were not happy, claiming that in general the Dutch beat and mistreated them when trading. After 1660 both Lambert and his wife Annetje disappear from the records.

With my permission the following Van Valkenburg research in chronological timeline format was published as *Lambert Van Valkenburg: His Life in the New World as Revealed in Court Documents and Other Primary Source Records From 1644 - 1664* by Lorine McGinnis Schulze, in <u>The National Association of the Van Valkenburg Family of America</u> serialized beginning in the Fall of 1999.

25 January 1644-29 June 1644: Lambert van Volackenborch (Valckenborch aka Valkenburg) from Valkenburg, Limurg, Netherlands, soldier, was on a roster of men who fought the Manhatten Indian War. [25]

25 January 1644: Declaration. Olof Stevensen (van Cortlandt) and Gysbert Opdyck as to a statement of Lambert van Valckenborch, respecting property of Peter Livesen, dec'd. (full particulars, in Dutch, may be consulted in Register of Provincial Secretary, Vol. II, p. 95) [26]

29 July 1644: Deed. Jan Jacobssen to Lambert van Valckenburgh, of house and plantation on the island of Manhattan, near Fort Amsterdam. [27]

16 March 1647: Patent. Lammert van Valckenborch; lot south of Fort Amsterdam, Manhattan Island. [28]

9 January 1657: Actions. Lambert van Valkenborch against. Hendrick Claessen and Gerrit Willemsen, for assault; put over. [29]

<u>Ordinary Session held in Fort Orange, **January 9 Anno 1657**</u>
President, J. La Montagne
Rutger Jacobsen
Jacob Schermerhoorn
Andries Herbertsen
Philip Pietersen
"Lambert van Valckenborch, plaintiff, against Henderick Claessen and Gerrit Willemsen, defendants. The plaintiff complains that the defendants beat him and his wife in his own house. The defendants deny it and claim that the plaintiff chased them with a naked rapier out of his house and pursued them to the center of the fort. The court orders the parties respectively to prove their assertions." [30]

<u>Extraordinary Session held in Fort Orange, **June 7 Anno 1657**</u>
Present, the magistrates of this court and the members of the court martial of the burgher guard.
President, Jacob Schermerhorn Hendrick Jochimsen, lieutenant
Captain Abraham Staets
Philip Pietersen

Adriaen Gerritsen
Lambert v: Valckenborch, sergeant
"Pieter Jacobsen Borsboom complains that last Sunday evening, being the 5th of June, sitting in front of the guardhouse of the burgher guard, where he was lodging by permission of the magistrates, Marten, the mason, came to him before the guard was set and asked him what had become of the candles? Whereupon he answered that he did not know; to which Marten replied: "You have taken them." The plaintiff answered: "You lie." Marten immediately drew his sword and cut the plaintiff's head as he made a move to get up.

Marten, the mason, being examined and asked why he wounded Pieter Van Borsboom, answers that he told him he lied and called him a rascal. Lambert van Valkenborch, sergeant of the burgher guard, who was present, says that on coming to the guard house he ordered a candle to be lit. Marten, the mason, stepping outside the guard house asked Pieter Jacobsen Borsboom where the candles were? To which question Pieter Jacobsen Borsboom answered: "I do not know." Marten replied: "You stole them." The aforesaid Pieter Jacobsen Borsboom then said: "You lie like a rascal and a knave." The aforesaid Marten then drew his sword and cut the said Pieter Jacobsen Borboom's head as he rose from his seat.

The court refers the matter to a committee of four, to wit, two from the court and two from the court martial, to render a decision in the case, namely, Jacob Schermerhoorn and Philip Pietersen Schuyler from the court and Captain Abraham Staets and Hendrick Jochimsen, lieutenant, from the burghers." [31]

4 September 1657: Actions. Mr. Van Hamel, secretary of Renselaweswyck against. Lambert van Valckenburgh, for loss sustained in the sale of a field of wheat on the farm of Jan Labite which he had purchased at auction, and which had to be resold for non-payment of purchase money; judgement for plaintiff with costs and damages. [32]

In court documents dated 1653 and 1658 at Fort Orange (present day Albany), New York, we see that Lambert owned land near Fort Orange:

"...a lot behind Fort Orange for a garden, bounded on the east side by Pieter jacobsen, on the north side by Lambert van Valckenborch, on the south and west sides by a road..." [33]
"... together with a lot behind Fort Orange for a garden, bounded on the east side by Pieter Jacobsen, on the north side by Lambert van Valckenborch [sic], on the south and west sides a road" [34]

Power of attorney from Lambert van Valckenborch to Govert Loockermans

[330] "Appeared before me, Johannes La Montagne in the service of the General Chartered West India Company commissary at Fort Orange and the village of Beverwyck, in presence of the hereinafter named witnesses, Lambert van Valckenborgh, who declares that he hereby constitutes and appoints the Honorable Govert Loockermans his attorney in the principal's name and on his behalf to demand and receive of Jan Dircksen alias de Schreder, a certain three and a half beavers due to him, the principal, from the aforesaid Jan Dircksz for house rent, promising to hold good whatever the attorney shall do in this matter, for which he binds his person and estate, real and personal, submitting the same to all courts and judges. Done in Fort Orange, the 28th of July AO. 1658. in presence of Fredrick Harmsen and J. Provoost, witnesses.
This is the X mark of LAMBERT VAN VALCKENBORCH, made by himself
This is the S E mark of Fredrick Harmsen
Johannes Provoost, witness
Acknowledged before me,
LA MONTAGNE, Commissary at Fort Orange" [35]

Extraordinary Session held in Fort Orange, **August 8 Anno 1659**
"Instructions issued by the honorable commissary and magistrates of Fort Orange and the village of Beverwyck for the rattle watch, appointed at the request of the burghers to relieve them of night-watch duty; to the rattle watch of which place Lambert van Valckenborgh and Pieter Winnen were appointed the 6th of July of this year 1659, on condition that they together are to receive for the term of one year one thousand and one hundred guilders in seawan and one hundred guilders in beavers.

First, the said rattle watch shall be held to appear at the burghers' guard house after the ringing of the nine o'clock bell and together at ten o'clock shall begin making their rounds, giving notice of their presence in all the streets of the village of Beverwyck by sounding their rattle and calling [out the hour], and this every hour of the night, until 4 o'clock in the morning.

Secondly, they shall pay especial attention to fire and upon the first sign of smoke, extraordinary light or otherwise warn the people by knocking at their houses. And if they see any likelihood of fire, they shall give warning by rattling and calling, and run to the church, of which they are to have a key, and ring the bell.

Thirdly, in case they find any thieves breaking into any houses or gardens, they shall to the best of their ability try to prevent it, arrest the thieves and bring them into the fort. And in case they are not strong enough to do so, they are to call the burghers of the vicinity to their aid, who are in duty bound to lend the helping hand, as this is tending to the common welfare.

Fourthly, in case of opposition, they are hereby authorized to offer resistance, the honorable commissary and magistrates declaring that they release them from all liability for any accident which may happen or result from such resistance if offered in the rightful performance of their official duties.

Which instructions the aforesaid rattle watch shall swear to observe. Actum in Fort Orange, the 3d of September Anno 1659." [36]

27 May 1660: Petition. Jan Dircksen van Bremen, Arent Jansen van Hoeck, Jan Harmsen, Rem Jansen, Lambert van Valckenburgh, Jan Jansen van Eeckelen, Peter Winne, Cornelis Borgardus, Philip Hendricksen, Hendrick Roseboom, Wynant Geritsen van de Poel and divers others, praying that Dutch as well as Indian brokers may be employed to trade with the Indians. [37]

17 June 1660: Order on the above petition, permitting the petitioners to act as in their discretion they may think fit, as some of them had openly avowed their intention to do so whether it was allowed them or not [38]

26 June 1660: Proposals of the Mohawks protesting against the employment of Dutch brokers in the woods, and complaining that they beat and otherwise ill treated the Indians [39]

28 June 1660: Advice and opinions of the several magistrates on the above proposals [40]

28 June 1660: Ordinance. Prohibiting the employment of Christians as brokers among the indians in the woods [41]

Ordinary Session held in Fort Orange, **June 1 Anno 1660**
Present:
La Montagne
Sander Leen[dersen]
Anderies Herpertsen
Evert Jansen Wendel
"Abrahm Carpeyn, plaintiff, against Immetie, the wife of Evert, the baker, defendant. The plaintiff complains that the defendant took linen and other goods from the house of Lambert van Valkenb[urg] that belonged to him. The defendant says that she took it on account of debt. The court condemns the plaintiff to pay the defendant and also orders the defendant to return the linen." [42]

LAMBERT VAN VALKENBURG'S SON JOCHEM LAMBERTSE VAN VALKENBURG

Jochem Lambertse Van Valkenburg was baptised in November 1646 in New Amsterdam (present day New York City). Not much is known of his early years although it is very likely that he settled in Kinderhook as a young man. Kinderhook records are few and far between, thus we cannot account for his early years. Sometime in the 1670s Jochem married Eva Hendrickse Vrooman, born in the Netherlands to Hendrick Meesen Vrooman and Jannetje Wouters.

Shortly after Jannetje's death, Eva Vrooman's father Hendrick and his five children ages 15, 13, 11, 7 and 5 years old sailed to the New World on the ship D'Eendracht (The Concord) arriving in New Amsterdam on 17 April 1664. Hendrick and his family settled first at Kinderhook, then Steen Raby [Lansingburg] and finally Schenectady in 1677.

Ten years after Eva's death in Kinderhook in 1706, Jochem married for the second time to Jannetie Thomasz Mingael, the widow of Lambert Van Alstyne. [43]

ISAAC THE LOYALIST'S GRANDFATHER, ISAAC JOCHEMSE VAN VALKENBURG

Jochem and Eva had ten children born between 1670 and 1695. Their 7th child, Isaac Jochemse Van Valkenburg, was baptised 4 July 1686 in Albany. [44] On 4 October 1705 Isaac married Lydia Van Slyke in Schenectady. [45] Lydia's grandmother was Ots-Toch, a Mohawk woman who married the Dutchman Cornelis Van Slyke in New Netherland. Lydia herself was born about 1686 in Schenectady [46] to Jacques Cornelise Van Slyke and Margarita (Grietje) Harmense Ryckman.

Isaac and Lydia had six children born in Schenectady, and it was their son Isaac Van Valkenburg who became the father of Isaac the Loyalist. With three generations of Isaacs it is important to distinguish them so I will refer to them as Isaac Sr (Isaac who married Lydia Van Slyke), Isaac the Patriot (Isaac the son of Isaac and Lydia) and Isaac the Loyalist (Isaac Van Valkenburg aka Vollick). Isaac the Patriot was baptised in Schenectady 13 February 1711 [47], the third of Isaac and Lydia's six children.

ISAAC THE LOYALIST'S FATHER, ISAAC VAN VALKENBURG

On 17 December 1732, Isaac the Loyalist was baptised in Schoharie as the illegitimate son of Maria Bradt. [48] Isaac's maternal grandparents, Isaac and Lydia Van Valkenburg, were the sponsors, indicating that the family acknowledged his Van Valkenburg paternity. His father's name is not given, indicating an illegitimate birth. Nothing more is known of Isaac's mother Maria after this 1732 date.

When little Isaac was 5, his father married Jannetje Clements. [49] Whether Isaac the Loyalist ever lived with them is not known. Isaac the Patriot and his wife Jannetje had several children in Albany but eventually settled in Wysox Pennsylvania. The book "A History of Bradford County Pennsylvania" provides some details:

The first settlement on the territory included in the present township of Wysox was made in 1776, by Isaac and Hermanas Van Valkenburg, and the sons-in-law of Isaac Van Valkenburg, Sebastian and Isaac Strope, who came from near Claverack, on the Hudson river, in the present county of Columbia (then Albany), New York, to the Indian meadows, or Miscuscim, near the present Frcnchtown railroad depot, in May, 1773.

On April 7, 1787, Isaac Van Valkenburg and Bastian Strope quitclaimed to William Ross, by deed, "a lot improved in May, 1773, lying on Miscuscim flat, two miles below the Standing Stone, and six miles above Wya-lusing."

Early in 1776, having bought a right in the Susquehanna company, they located it in Wysox, and moved upon the lower part of the flats, their house standing on the west side of the Wysox creek and near its mouth, a short distance southeast of the present residence of Dr. Madill. Under date of Feb. 17, 1776, Capt. Solomon Strong sells to Isaac and "Harmanos" Van Valkenburg and to "Bostian" Strope each one-half share in the Susquehanna company's purchase, which the grantor bought of Samuel Hogskiss and Daniel Lawrence, they being original proprietors. The settlement was made some time before the survey and according to the rules of the company the family had the land due them on their right surveyed to them where they located.

The family consisted of Isaac Van Valkenburg and his wife; Herman Van Valkenburg, a brother of Isaac, who was a bachelor and died unmarried; Sebastian Strope, whose wife, Lydia, was a daughter of Isaac Van Valkenburg, and John Strope, who married another daughter of Isaac; and another daughter who was unmarried, and probably a son, John Van Valkenburg. It is probable that Herman died before the captivity of the family by the Indians. Isaac Van Valkenburg and his wife died in Wysox, after their return to the township, after the war closed, which was about 1785.

We give a few incidents concerning the captivity of the Strope family, which are not contained in the general narrative in Chapter III. When the family were captured, they took away with them the old Dutch family Bible. The Indians threw the Bible into the fire, but Mrs. Strope plucked it out after it had been somewhat damaged. Henry Tuttle, of Wysox, the husband of Mary Strope, granddaughter of the lady who rescued the book, has the same now in his possession. Mrs. Sebastian Strope was subjected to many trials during her captivity, none of which were more distressing than the following: she was made the victim of her tormentors in their horrid sport, who, taking advantage of her anxiety to learn the fate of her husband, told her, as they brought in the reeking scalps of the settlers they had slain, that "Boss Johns" (as they called Sebastian, a corruption of Bostian) scalp was among them. She made frequent examinations of the bloody trophies to see if, indeed, their fiendish stories were true.

Besides the family of Sebastian, his brother, called "Big John" Strope, his wife and children, were also taken prisoners, and, when the exchange was effected, he was not included in the cartel. When he returned, his person showed scars and ca!losities made by the tortures he had endured. He was a man of large frame and indomitable will, and suffered the persecutions of his tormentors like a martyr. [50]

On 7 April 1787 *"Isaac VanVolkenburg now living at Wyasock in Luzerne County"* quit claimed to William Ross, by deed for the sum of £5, *"Land Improved in May seventeen hundred seventy three Lying in Missushum flat about Two miles below Standing Stone & six miles above Wyalusing and scituate on the east Branch of Susquehannah river and on the West side of said Branch."* Signed *"Isaac VanVolkenburgh."* [51]

Isaac was a Patriot who was captured by Indians during the American Revolution and taken to Quebec where he was held prisoner for 5 years. The narrative of his granddaughter Jane Strope, captured with the family, provides a compelling account of their capture. Her cousin Polly Strope's obituary also gives us details.

Jane Strope's narrative states *"my mother and her six children, including myself, were made captives by the Indians on the 20th day of May, previous to the Massacre (1778). My grandparents who had come with my father from Catskill, were also captured."*

The obituary of Polly Strope reads *"He (Isaac VanValkenburg) and his son-in-law John Strope, were for a time confined in Fort Niagara, where an attempt was made to convert the latter to the cause of King George. He resisted all their reasoning and promises. Acting upon the Gnostie principle, that evil resides in matter, they attempted to expel it by the ordeal of starvation. For this purpose they kept him five successive days without food or drink. As he afterwards remarked, he thought he should die under it. The want of food was not very distressing, but for the want of drink he suffered amazingly – and that suffering was aggravated, if possible, by the sight of a pure flowing brook in front of his window! But in his case, as in may others at that day, the principles of liberty proved to be more inveterate in the colonists than any mere physical disorder, and no system of diet could eradicate them. Finding their efforts in vain, they desisted before the spark of life was quite extinguished. After a captivity of about five years they were exchanged, and returned to their original home, to obtain, wherewith to commence again on the land they had more recently left."*

Jane Strope further stated, *"They took us at once to Tioga Point. There they gave us as prisoners to the English under Butler." "The Indians and other forces and all the prisoners, including myself, went up the Susquehanna to Bainbridge, and some went to Unadilla, which the Indians called Teunadilla. This was in the latter part of the summer or perhaps in July. We were in that vicinity several weeks. We remained there three weeks, then we went to Tioga Point in canoes. We remained at Tioga Point sometime until Col. Hartley's victory over the Indians. All the captives were sent off up the Chemung on their way to Fort Niagara under an Indian escort. After reaching the lake (Ontario), part of the company went by land and part by water to Fort Niagara."*

"We were at the Fort three weeks, then were put aboard of an English vessel and sailed for Bucks Island. We went from Bucks Island in batteaux down the St. Lawrence to a place called Sorel. Thence to Lachine, not far from Montreal. It was winter when we reached Lachine. From Lachine we were carried to a place called St. Johns where we remained as prisoners two years and nine months. From that place we were sent to Three Rivers Point where the settlement was called Machust. From thence on our people making application to the Gov. we had the privilege of going back to the neighborhood of Montreal, which we did on the 1st of May, 1781 performing the journey the most of the way on the ice. We remained at or near Montreal until August of that year."

"In the Spring of the next year, after peace was declared (The Treaty of Paris, signed on September 3, 1783, ratified by Congress on January 14, 1784, and by the King of Great Britain on April 9, 1784 formally ended the American Revolutionary War) her father and brother came on to Wysox, and in the Fall the family and relatives joined them. They found everything had been burned that could be fired. Their cattle had all been made booty of and everything of value plundered." [52]

The Van Slyke Family

Isaac the Loyalist's Van Slyke Ancestry

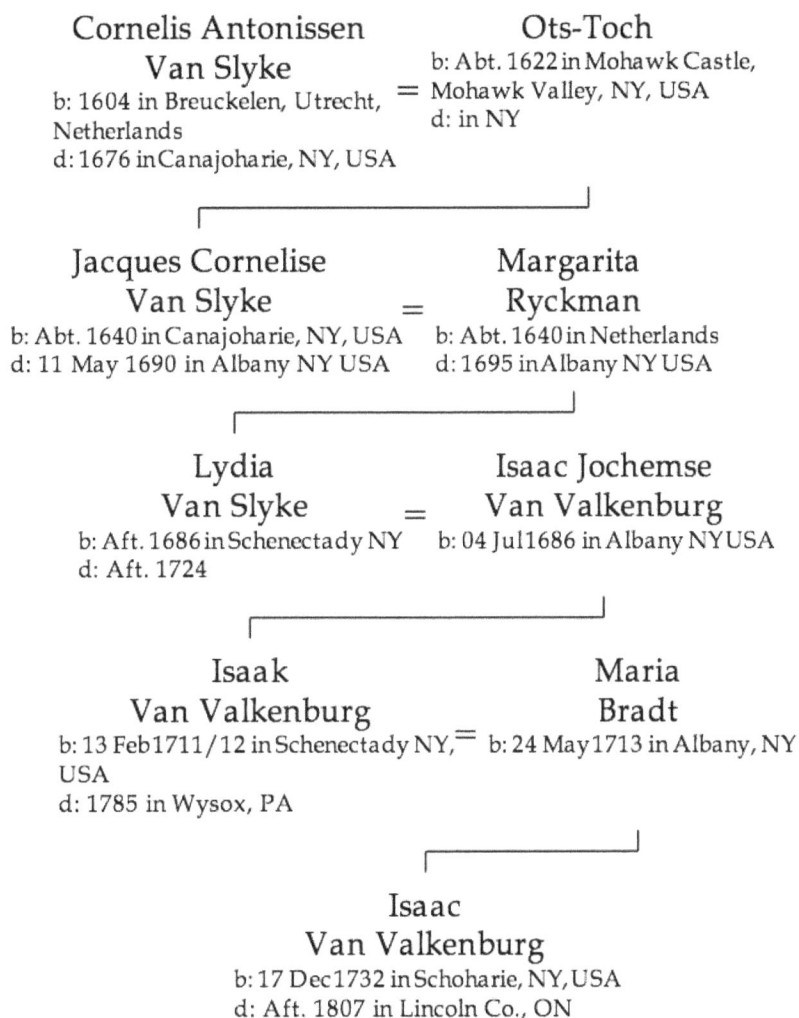

Cornelis Antonissen Van Slyke
b: 1604 in Breuckelen, Utrecht, Netherlands
d: 1676 in Canajoharie, NY, USA

=

Ots-Toch
b: Abt. 1622 in Mohawk Castle, Mohawk Valley, NY, USA
d: in NY

Jacques Cornelise Van Slyke
b: Abt. 1640 in Canajoharie, NY, USA
d: 11 May 1690 in Albany NY USA

=

Margarita Ryckman
b: Abt. 1640 in Netherlands
d: 1695 in Albany NY USA

Lydia Van Slyke
b: Aft. 1686 in Schenectady NY
d: Aft. 1724

=

Isaac Jochemse Van Valkenburg
b: 04 Jul 1686 in Albany NY USA

Isaak Van Valkenburg
b: 13 Feb 1711/12 in Schenectady NY, USA
d: 1785 in Wysox, PA

=

Maria Bradt
b: 24 May 1713 in Albany, NY

Isaac Van Valkenburg
b: 17 Dec 1732 in Schoharie, NY, USA
d: Aft. 1807 in Lincoln Co., ON

For further details on the Van Slyke family please consult *The Van Slyke Family in America: A Genealogy of Cornelise Antonissen Van Slyke, 1604-1676 and his Mohawk Wife Ots-Toch, including the story of Jacques Hertel, 1603-1651, Father of Ots-Toch and Interpreter to Samuel de Champlain REVISED EDITION* by Lorine McGinnis Schulze published May 2010.

Mary Warner's Palatine Ancestors

Direct Descendants of Andreas Werner

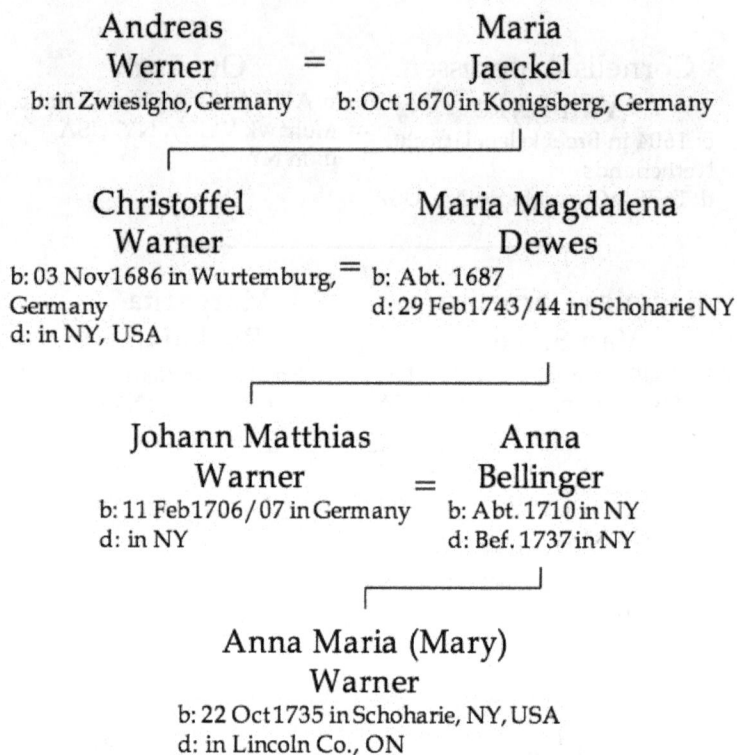

Andreas Werner = **Maria Jaeckel**
b: in Zwiesigho, Germany | b: Oct 1670 in Konigsberg, Germany

Christoffel Warner = **Maria Magdalena Dewes**
b: 03 Nov 1686 in Wurtemburg, Germany
d: in NY, USA | b: Abt. 1687
d: 29 Feb 1743/44 in Schoharie NY

Johann Matthias Warner = **Anna Bellinger**
b: 11 Feb 1706/07 in Germany
d: in NY | b: Abt. 1710 in NY
d: Bef. 1737 in NY

Anna Maria (Mary) Warner
b: 22 Oct 1735 in Schoharie, NY, USA
d: in Lincoln Co., ON

Mary's father Matthias Warner was born 11 February 1707 in Germany to Christoffel Warner and Maria Magadlena (Magadalena) Dewes. He would have been about 2 or 3 years old when his family fled the Palatine area of Germany to come to New York and a new life.

HISTORY OF THE PALATINES [53]

The Palatinate or German Pfalz was, in German history, the land of the Count Palatine, a title held by a leading secular prince of the Holy Roman Empire. Geographically, the Palatinate was divided between two small territorial clusters: the Rhenish, or Lower Palatinate, and the Upper Palatinate. The Rhenish Palatinate included lands on both sides of the Middle Rhine River between its Main and Neckar tributaries. Its capital until the 18th century was Heidelberg. The Upper Palatinate was located in northern Bavaria, on both sides of the Naab River as it flows south toward the Danube and extended eastward to the Bohemian Forest. The boundaries of the Palatinate varied with the political and dynastic fortunes of the Counts Palatine.

The Palatinate has a border beginning in the north, on the Moselle River about 35 miles southwest of Coblenz to Bingen and east to Mainz, down the Rhine River to Oppenheim, Guntersblum and Worms, then continuing eastward above the Nieckar River about 25 miles east of Heidelberg then looping back westerly below Heidelberg to Speyer, south down the Rhine River to Alsace, then north-westerly back up to its beginning on the Moselle River.

The first Count Palatine of the Rhine was Hermann I, who received the office in 945. Although not originally hereditary, the title was held mainly by his descendants until his line expired in 1155, and the Bavarian Wittelsbachs took over in 1180. In 1356, the Golden Bull (a papal bull: an official document, usually commands from the Pope and sealed with the official Papal seal called a Bulla) made the Count Palatine an Elector of the Holy Roman Empire. During the Reformation, the Palatinate accepted Protestantism and became the foremost Calvinist region in Germany.

After Martin Luther published his 95 Theses on the door of the castle church at Wittenberg on 31 October 1517, many of his followers came under considerable religious persecution for their beliefs. Perhaps for reasons of mutual comfort and support, they gathered in what is known as the Palatine. These folk came from many places, Germany, Holland, Switzerland and beyond, but all shared a common view on religion.

The protestant Elector Palatine Frederick V (1596-1632), called the "Winter King" of Bohemia, played a unique role in the struggle between Roman Catholic and Protestant Europe. His election in 1619 as King of Bohemia precipitated the Thirty Years War that lasted from 1619 until 1648. Frederick was driven from Bohemia and in 1623, deposed as Elector Palatine.

During the Thirty Years War, the Palatine country and other parts of Germany suffered from the horrors of fire and sword as well as from pillage and plunder by the French armies. This war was based upon both politics and religious hatreds, as the Roman Catholic armies sought to crush the religious freedom of a politically-divided Protestantism.

Many unpaid armies and bands of mercenaries, both of friends and foe, devoured the substance of the people and by 1633 even the catholic French supported the Elector Palatine for a time for political reasons.

During the War of the Grand Alliance (1689-97), the troops of the French monarch Louis XIV ravaged the Rhenish Palatinate, causing many Germans to emigrate. Many of the early German settlers of America (e.g. the Pennsylvania Dutch) were refugees from the Palatinate. During the French Revolutionary and Napoleonic Wars, the Palatinate's lands on the west bank of the Rhine were incorporated into France, while its eastern lands were divided largely between neighbouring Baden and Hesse.

Nearly the entire 17th century in central Europe was a period of turmoil as Louis XIV of France sought to increase his empire. The War of the Palatinate (as it was called in Germany), aka The War of The League of Augsburg, began in 1688 when Louis claimed the Palatinate. Every large city on the Rhine above Cologne was sacked. The War ended in 1697 with the Treaty of Ryswick. The Palatinate was badly battered but still outside French control. In 1702, the War of the Spanish Succession began in Europe and lasted until 1713, causing a great deal of instability for the Palatines. The Palatinate lay on the western edge of the Holy Roman Empire not far from France's eastern boundary. Louis wanted to push his eastern border to the Rhine, the heart of the Palatinate.

While the land of the Palatinate was good for its inhabitants, many of whom were farmers, vineyard operators etc., its location was unfortunately subject to invasion by the armies of Britain, France, and Germany. Mother Nature also played a role in what happened, for the winter of 1708 was particularly severe and many of the vineyards perished. So, as well as the devastating effects of war, the Palatines were subjected to the winter of 1708-09, the harshest in 100 years.

The scene was set for a mass migration. At the invitation of Queen Anne in the spring of 1709, about 7000 harassed Palatines sailed down the Rhine to Rotterdam. From there, about 3000 were dispatched to America, either directly or via England, under the auspices of William Penn. The remaining 4000 were sent via England to Ireland to strengthen the protestant interest.

Although the Palatines were scattered as agricultural settlers over much of Ireland, major accumulations were found in Counties Limerick and Tipperary. As the years progressed and dissatisfactions increased, many of these folk seized opportunities to join their compatriots in Pennsylvania, or to go to newly-opened settlements in Canada.

There were many reasons for the desire of the Palatines to emigrate to the New World: oppressive taxation, religious bickering, hunger for more and better land, the advertising of the English colonies in America and the favourable attitude of the British government toward settlement in the North American colonies. Many of the Palatines believed they were going to Pennsylvania, Carolina or one of the tropical islands.

The passage down the Rhine took from 4 to 6 weeks. Tolls and fees were demanded by authorities of the territories through which they passed. Early in June, the number of Palatines entering Rotterdam reached 1000 per week. Later that year, the British government issued a Royal proclamation in German that all arriving after October 1709 would be sent back to Germany. The British could not effectively handle the number of Palatines in London and there may have been as many as 32000 by November 1709. They wintered over in England since there were no adequate arrangements for the transfer of the Palatines to the English colonies.

In 1710, three large groups of Palatines sailed from London. The first went to Ireland, the second to Carolina and the third to New York with the new Governor, Robert Hunter. There were 3000 Palatines on 10 ships that sailed for New York and approximately 470 died on the voyage or shortly after their arrival. What is referred to as the Hunter Lists was created from these Palatines who came to New York.

In New York, the Palatines were expected to work for the British authorities, producing naval stores [tar and pitch] for the navy in return for their passage to New York. They were also expected to act as a buffer between the French and Natives on the northern frontier and the English colonies to the south and east.

These Palatine refugees in New York were not treated well. They could not own land, had few, if any, rights, and basically were treated as slaves. Their children were frequently taken from them and forced to work as servants and child apprentices in homes far away.

THE PALATINE WARNER FAMILY

Christoph Werner who was born in Wurtemburg Germany in Nov 1686 was #805 on the Hunter Lists of New York. He was only one name from Michael Werner on the Hunter Subsistence Rolls on 4 Aug. 1710. Since the lists were not in alpha order, there was likely a relationship between the two men. Christoph probably came from Rheinfels as did Michael. Christoff Werner age 33, wife and son age 1, Lutheran husbandman and Vinedresser, were in the first arrivals of Palatines in England in 1709.

Christoph made his first appearance on the Hunter Lists on 4 Aug. 1710 with 2 people over 10 years and one person under 10 in his household. On 24 December 1711 the family consisted of 2 persons over 10 and 2 under 10.

Christoph Werner, 35, and Maria Magdalena Werner age 23, and John Matheus Werner age 3 were in New York City in 1710. He was naturalized on 13 March 1715 in Albany. Christoph Werner and Magdalena with 3 children were at NeuStuttgardt in 1716.

Christoph Werner married Maria Magdalena Dewes, who joined the Lutheran Church at Newtown on 12 June 1712. She appeared on Pastor Sommer's family List at Schoharie circa 1744. She died 29 Feb. 1744 age 57 years in Schoharie.

Matthias Warner, their son, was on Pastor Sommer's Family List at Schoharie circa 1744 with his offspring. Matthias Warner married first Anna Bellinger circa 1730. They had four children, including Mary Warner who later married Isaac Van Valkenburg aka Vollick. Matthias married secondly Anna's sister, Maria Barbara Bellinger about 1737. They had seven children.

The Bradt Family

The brothers Albert Andriess de Norman (1607c.-1686) and Arent Andriesse first emigrated as early as 1630, and were among the early settlers at Rensselaerswyck. They came from Fredrikstad, a town at the mouth of the Glommen, the largest river in Norway.

Albert Andriess, known as "de Noorman" (the Norwegian) was a land owner and tobacco farmer at Bushwick, New York in August 1630. He established himself a few miles south of Albany on a stream called "Norman's Kil," where he built a mill.

He married first to Annetie Barents von Rolmers. Albert Andriessen apparently returned to Holland (perhaps on business), for on 26 August 1636, the following contract was signed at Amsterdam, Netherlands:

"In the name of the Lord, Amen. On conditions hereafter specified, we, Pieter Cornelissen van munnickendam, millwright, 43 years of age, Claesz jans van naerden, 33 years of age, house carpenter, and albert andriessen van fredrickstadt, 29 years of age, tobacco planter, have agreed among ourselves, first to sail in God's name to New Netherland in the small vessel which now lies ready and to betake ourselves to the colony of Rensselaerswyck for the purpose of settling there on the following conditions made with Mr. Kiliaen Van Rensselaer, as patroon of the said colony, etc.

Thus done and passed in good faith, under pledge of our persons and property subject to all courts and justices for the fulfillment of what is aforewritten, at Amsterdam, this 26th of August 1636.

In witness whereof we have signed these with our own hands in the presence of the undersigned notary public . . . .

Killiaen Van Rensselaer
Pieter Cornelissen
albert andriessen [sic]
Claes Jansen
J.Vande Ven, Notary."

He sailed from Trexel on 8 October 1636 accompanied by his wife, Annetje Barents of Rolmers, two children and his brother, Arent Andriessen on the ship Rensselaerswyck, which arrived at New Amsterdam, 4 March 1637. The voyage was through rough seas, and a son born to his wife during the voyage was named Storm. The log of the ship contains under the date of Sunday, 2 November 1636, the following entry:

"Drifted 16 leagues N.E. by E.; the wind about west, the latitude by dead reconing 41 degrees, 50 min. with very high seas. That day the overhang above our rudder was

knocked in by severe storm. This day a child was born on the ship, and named and baptized in England stoerm; the mother is annetie baernts. This day gone."

This child, Storm, eventually took the surname Vanderzee (from the sea) and his descendants are known by this name. The rest of Albert and Annetje's children took the surname Bradt, as did Albert himself.

In a letter of 10 May 1638 to Albert, Van Rensselaer acknowledged that he had received a letter from Albert stating that the tobacco looked fine; but he was desirous to get full particulars, including a sample of the tobacco. He also informed him that he had heard from several people that he was *"very unmerciful to his children and very cruel"* to his wife; and he was to avoid this *"and in all things have the fear of the Lord"* before his eyes and not follow so much in his own inclinations.

The patroon had several disagreements with the brothers, Albert and Arent over their accounting practices and operation of the tobacco plantation; however, they apparently were showing a profit for the patroon, so he seems to have tolerated them.

Albert acquired a house and lot from Hendrick Kip on 29 August 1651. It lay northeast of Fort Amsterdam. On 5 October 1655, he was taxed fl. 20 for this house and lot. [Register of Provincial Secretary Vol. III p. 92] [Source: Calendar of Historical Manuscripts in the office of the Secretary of State, Albany New York edited by EB O'Callaghan]

Albert not only cultivated tobacco, he operated two large sawmills, run by a powerful waterfall. From 4 May 1652 to 4 May 1672, he is charged by the patroon with the annual rent for these two mills and the land on Norman's Kill.

In May 1655, Roeloff Jansen, a butcher, appeared before the court of the Burgomasters and Schepens in New Amsterdam, and made a complaint against Christiaen Barentsen, attorney for Albert Andriessen. Jansen had leased a house and some land belonging to Albert, who was to give him some cows. But the house was "not tight" and "not enclosed," and the cows were missing. Albert was ordered to make repairs.

Albert Andriessen's first wife Annetie died before 5 June 1662, and he then married Pietertie Jansen.

Albert was in and out of trouble for much of his life. In his later years he was found guilty in court of trying to burn down his son's house with his son inside, of setting fire to a neighbour's field, of beating his first wife so badly she required a surgeon's care, and of behaving inappropriately towards the children in the neighbourhood. At one point the court ordered his sons to keep him under control. He and his third wife, Geertury Coeymans, divorced and carried on a volatile relationship during settlement cases that were heard in the courts. Albert died 7 June 1686.

ALBERT'S FIRST WIFE, ANNETIE BARENTS (VAN) ROTTMER AND HER MOTHER, GEESIE BARENTSDR.

Gissel or Geesie Barentsdr. [Barentsdochter] assisted her daughter Annatie Barents Van Rottmer at the signing of banns on 27 March 1632 for her marriage to Albert Andriessen. Annetie was 24 years old. When Annatie's brother Barent Barents signed his banns at the age of 22, on 21 April 1632 he too was assisted by his mother. At the time Gissel was living on the Schaepensteegje or Sheep Alley in Amsterdam, Netherlands. Geesie's husband Barent Rottmer is never listed, so it is assumed he died before 1632.

When Geesie Barents came to New Netherland on board "Den Waterhondt" in the fall of 1640 her husband Barent Rottmer was dead. By the end of 1640 she had married Pieter Jacobse Van Rynsburgh, whether in Holland or not is not known. Pieter was probably the West India Company gunner at Fort Orange.

The passenger list shows Gijsje Berents, wife of Pieter Jacobsz. Gijsje was charged with board on den Waterhondt in 1640 and credited with 28 days work done by her husband at the home of Arent van Curler. Pieter Jacobsz may have been the "constapel" of Fort Orange, who on 15 April 1652 by order of Johannes Dyckman, tore van Slichtenhorst's proclamation from the house of Gijsbert Cornelisz, tavern keeper.

Geesie and Pieter filed a joint will in New Amsterdam in June 1642 leaving all of their separate estates to each other. If Geesie died first, Pieter was to pay her daughter Annatie, twenty carolus guilders. Since Pieter made the first of three payments to the deacons of Fort Orange for an adult funeral pall, on 12 April 1658, it appears that Geesie had died that previous winter or spring.

Geesie's daughter, Annetie Bradt, appears to have died early in 1661 since a payment for a pall was made on 13 February that year.

GENERATION 2: JAN ALBERTSEN BRADT CA 1648-1697 MARRIED MARIA POST

Jan seems to have been a quiet, well-behaved son and little is found about him in the early records of New Netherland. The last time Jan appears in the church records is May 23, 1697 when he stood as sponsor at the baptism of Maria, daughter of Cornelis Van Slyke and Clara Bradt. In the Albany Census taken June 1697 his widow Maria Post is shown as a widow with 5 children.

Maria was born and baptised in Recife Brazil to Captain Adriaen Crijnen Post and his wife Clara Moockers in June 1649. [54] By the time Brazil fell to the Portuguese in 1654, the family had returned to the Netherlands. By 1655 they were on Staten Island where Adriaen was put in charge of a small colony. On 15 September 1655 the colony on Staten Island was burned to the ground by the Natives from

Hackensack. Twenty-three people were killed and sixty-seven taken prisoner, among them Adrien, his wife, five children, and two servants. They family were eventually released.

GENERATION 3: STORM BRADT B. 1689 MARRIED SOPHIA UZIELE B. 1691

Sophia was descended from French Walloons and Huguenots who fled religious persecution.

GENERATION 4: MARIA BRADT MOTHER OF ISAAC VOLLICK THE LOYALIST

Nothing is known of Maria except that she baptised her illegitimate son Isaac with his paternal grandparents standing as sponsors.

The Loyalist Isaac Van Valkenburg aka Vollick & His Children

Maretje Vollick was baptised 28 May 1758 in Albany, New York [55]. No further information.

Matthias Valck was baptised 17 June 1759 in Schoharie, New York, USA [56]. He married **Baertie Bradt** 04 January 1786 in Albany, New York, USA [57], daughter of David Bradt and Treyntje Lang. She was baptised 23 April 1758 in Albany, New York, USA [58]. He is believed to have returned to New York after his family settled in Niagara.

Cornelius Vollick was baptised 16 Aug 1761 in Albany New York [59], and died after 1818 in Ontario. He married **Eve Larroway** 24 Mar 1795 in Niagara, Ontario [60], daughter of the Loyalist Jonas Larroway and Elizabeth Muller. She was baptised 14 Mar 1776 in Berne, Albany Co. New York.

Annaje Vollick was baptised 26 June 1763 in Schoharie, New York, USA[61], and died before 1823 in Ontario. She married **Derrick (Richard) Hainer** about 1783 in Niagara, Ontario, son of Henry Hainer. He was born about 1759 in New York, and died 1801 in Ontario.

Storm Follick was baptised 17 February 1765 in Schoharie, New York, USA [62], and died after 1828. He married **Esther** (surname unknown) after September 1787 in Ontario. She was born about 1770.

Sophia Vollick was baptised 11 April 1766 in Schoharie New York USA [63]. She married **Adrian Bradt** before 1784 in Niagara Ontario, son of Albert Bradt and Magdalene Lang. He was baptised 14 August 1765 in Albany New York USA.

Elizabeth Vollick was baptised December 1767 in Schoharie, New York, USA [64]. She married **Christian Bradt** before 1784 in Niagara, Ontario. He was born 1763.

Catharina Vollick was baptised 25 June 1769 in Schoharie, New York, USA [65]. She married **Albert Hainer** after 1784 in Niagara, Ontario [66], son of Henry Hainer. He was born about 1758 in Near Albany New York, and died 2 July 1813.

Sarah Vollick was born 1770 in New York USA. She married **Benoni Crumb** between 14 December 1786 and 17 September 1787 in Niagara, Ontario. He was baptised in Minisink New York in 1760 as the illegitimate son of Lydia Krom.

John Vollick aka Van Valkenburg was baptised 25 July 1772 in Beaverdam, New York, USA [67]. He married **Sarah DeCow** 20 October 1798 in Niagara, Ontario, daughter of Jacob DeCoe and Elizabeth Bloome.

Possibly **Maria Vollick**, born 1775.

Endnotes

[1] Dutch Reformed Church of Schoharie NY: Dec. 17 1732. Mother Maria Bradden [sic] daughter of Storm. Child Isaac Falkenburg. Sponsors: Isaac Falkenburg and his wife Lydia

[2] The Mark of Honour by Hazel C. Mathews, University of Toronto Press 1965

[3] P.A.C., Colonial Office Records, M.G. 11, "Q" ser., vol. 13, p.331

[4] Great Britain, British Library, Additional Manuscripts, No. 21765, folios 64-65. p. 176, Appendix B

[5] Great Britain, British Library, Additional Manuscripts, No. 21765, folios 50-51

[6] Upper Canada Land Board Minutes and Records. RG1, L4, Vol. 5. Nassau District Minutes 1790-1794. pp16-18

[7] Abstract Index to Deeds

[8] Heir & Devisee Committee, Claim #39

[9] RG1 Series C-IV, MS 658 Reel 256 page 0131 4 April 1797

[10] Upper Canada Land Board Minutes and Records, RG1 L4 Vol. 5 Nassau District Minutes 1790-1794

[11] Upper Canada Land Board Minutes and Records RG1 L4 Vol. 6 Nassau District Schedule of Grants in Newark 1793-1794

[12] The documents extend into 8 pages and can be found on MS658 Reel 256 RG1 Series C-IV: Land Records 1783-1870 Pages 0119 to 0126 inclusive.

[13] The Holland Society, Baptism Record Albany Reformed Church, 1683-1804, Isaac Valk, Mareytje Warner - Mareytje. Sponsors Pieter Brat, Catarientje Brat.

[14] Transcribed and Indexed by Arthur C. M. Kelly, Baptism Record St. Paul's Lutheran Church 1728-1800 (Name: 1977;), Schoharie Lutheran #485 Parents Isac Falck, Maria. Child Matthes born 6 Dec. 1759 no bpt date. Wit. Matthes Werner, Catharina Zahe.

[15] The Holland Society, Baptism Record Albany Reformed Church, 1683-1804, 16 Aug. 1761: His baptismal record shows parents as Izak Valk and Marytje. Cornelia (this is obviously an error on the part of the transcriber, with the male name Cornelis being rendered incorrectly, the final "s" mistaken for an "a", as Cornelia). Sponsors Coenraad Hoogtelling and Cornelia Hoogtelling.

[16] Transcribed and Indexed by Arthur C. M. Kelly, Baptism Record St. Paul's Lutheran Church 1728-1800 (Name: 1977;), Schoharie Lutheran #680 Parents Isac Falk, Maria Child Annaje, bpt 26 June 1763. Wit. Matthes Werner jr, Eva Zahen.

[17] Transcribed and Indexed by Arthur C. M. Kelly, Baptism Record St. Paul's Lutheran Church 1728-1800 (Name: 1977;), Schoharie Lutheran #810. Parents Isac Falk, Maria. Chid Sturm [sic] born 17 Feb 1765, bpt 19 Feb 1765 Wit Nehrich Werner, Catharina Zahen.

[18] Transcribed and Indexed by Arthur C. M. Kelly, Baptism Record St. Paul's Lutheran Church 1728-1800 (Name: 1977;), Schoharie Lutheran #923. Parents Jost [sic] Falck, Maria. Child Sophia born 11 Apr. 1766 no bpt date. Wit Johannes Werner and wife.

[19] Transcribed and Indexed by Arthur C. M. Kelly, Baptism Record St. Paul's Lutheran Church 1728-1800 (Name: 1977;), Schoharie Lutheran #1042. Parents Isac Falck, Maria. Child Elisabeth born Dec. 1767 no bpt date. Wit. Christopher Werner and wife.

[20] Transcribed and Indexed by Arthur C. M. Kelly, Baptism Record St. Paul's Lutheran Church 1728-1800 (Name: 1977;), Schoharie Lutheran #1101. Parents Isac Falck, Maria. Child Catharina b. 25 June 1769 no bpt date. Wit. ____ Brath and wife.

[21] NYGBR Vol. 112, Number 2 April 1981

[22] Henry B. Hoff quotes from De Nederlandsche Leeuw of January-February 1980 regarding this Dutch ancestry of the Van Valkenburg(h) family

[23] Patronymic: Naming system based on father's first name

[24] Parents at baptism Reformed Dutch Church, NY, NY: Lambert Van Valckenburg (no mother named) Sponsors: Marten Cregier, Jan Hartman, Lyntie Jochems

[25] New Netherland Connections, Vol. 4 #4 p 188 by Jeff Snedeker

[26] Calendar of Historical Manuscripts in the office of the Secretary of State, Albany NY edited by EB O'Callaghan

[27] Register of Provincial Secretary Vol. II p. 121. Calendar of Historical Manuscripts in the office of the Secretary of State, Albany NY edited by EB O'Callaghan

[28] Land Papers Vol. G.G. p. 192. Calendar of Historical Manuscripts in the office of the Secretary of State, Albany NY edited by EB O'Callaghan

[29] Fort Orange Records, Vol. XVI p. 33. Calendar of Historical Manuscripts in the office of the Secretary of State, Albany NY edited by EB O'Callaghan

[30] Minutes of the Court of Fort Orange and Beverwyck 1657-1660, translated and edited by A.J.F. Van Laer, Vol.2, Albany, 1923. Page 9

[31] Minutes of the Court of Fort Orange and Beverwyck 1657-1660, translated and edited by A.J.F. Van Laer, Vol.2, Albany, 1923 Pages 40 - 41

[32] Fort Orange Records Vol. XVI p. 110-112. Calendar of Historical Manuscripts in the office of the Secretary of State, Albany NY edited by EB O'Callaghan

[33] 1653 deed from Willem Hofmeyer to Jochem Wesselsen, the baker not executed until 7 Oct. 1658

[34] 1658 deed from Jochem Wesselsen, the baker to Adriaen Jansen van Ilpendam, not executed

[35] Early Records of the City and County of Albany and Colony of Rensselaerswyck, vol. 4 (Mortgages 1658-1660; Wills 1681-1765) translated by Jonathan Pearson, revised and edited by A.J.F. Van Laer

[36] Minutes of the Court of Fort Orange and Beverwyck 1657-1660, translated and edited by A.J.F. Van Laer, Vol.2, Albany, 1923: Page 209-210:

[37] p. 169 Fort Orange Records Vol. XVI provides a full account

[38] p. 171 Fort Orange Records Vol. XVI provides a full account

[39] p. 172 Fort Orange Records Vol. XVI provides a full account

[40] p. 173 Fort Orange Records Vol. XVI provides a full account

[41] p. 175 Fort Orange Records Vol. XVI provides a full account. Calendar of Historical Manuscripts in the office of the Secretary of State, Albany NY edited by EB O'Callaghan

[42] Minutes of the Court of Fort Orange and Beverwyck 1657-1660, translated and edited by A.J.F. Van Laer, Vol.2, Albany, 1923: Page 257

[43] The Holland Society, Marriage Record Albany Reformed Church, 1683-1804. 1716, Feb. 23. After three Banns. Jochum Van Valkenburg, widr. of Eva Vroman, and Jannetie Mingaal, wid. of Lamberd Van Aalsteyn

[44] Baptismal record Albany DRC 1686: Jochum Van Valkenborg. Isaac (child). Sponsors Jacob Vosburg, Anna Jans

[45] New York Genealogical & Biographical Record, "First Dutch Reformed Church of Schenectady NY," Vol. LXXIII. #1. p. 37, 1705. Oct. 4. Isaak Valkenborg and Lydia van Slyk j.d. Banns called on 12 May 1704.

[46] The Schenectady church records were lost in the Schenectady Massacre of February 1690 when the French and Indians from Canada attacked and burned the little settlement.

[47] Schenectady DRC. Parents at baptism: Isaak Valkenburg, Lidia Van Slyk. Sponsors: Cornelis van Slyk, Claartjen Brat

[48] Sponsors at Isaac's baptism in the High and Low Dutch Church in Schoharie were Isaac and Lydia Falkenburg [sic] his paternal grandparents.

[49] Albany DRC. 28 May 1737

[50] Craft, The Reverend David; 1770-1878 History of Bradford County, Pennsylvania with Illustrations and Biographical Sketches of Some of its Prominient Men and Pioneers, originally published 1878 by L. H. Everts & Co., Philadelphia

[51] Exploring the Wysocton Capture by J. Kelsey Jones 2010. Luzerne Deed 2:459

[52] Exploring the Wysocton Capture by J. Kelsey Jones 2010. Jane Strope's narration, taken by Judge C. P. Avery of Owego, New York ca 1850

[53] previously published online at http://olivetreegenealogy.com/pal/overview.shtml and with permission, as Irish Palatine Story on the Internet in Irish Palatine Association Journal No. 7 December 1996

[54] C.J. Wasch, Doopregister der Hollanders in Brazilie 1633-1654. Adriaen Crijnen Post, Clara Moockers. Wt Christoffel ---, Andelijina Caron, Dorothea Montanier.

[55] The Holland Society, Baptism Record Albany Reformed Church, 1683-1804, Isaac Valk, Mareytje Warner - Mareytje. Sponsors Pieter Brat, Catarientje Brat

[56] Transcribed and Indexed by Arthur C. M. Kelly, Baptism Record St. Paul's Lutheran Church 1728-1800, (1977), Schohaire Lutheran #485 Parents Isac Falck, Maria. Child Matthes born 6 Dec. 1759 no bpt date. Wit. Matthes Werner, Catharina Zahe.

[57] Albany Reformed Dutch Church

[58] Albany Reformed Dutch Church

[59] The Holland Society, Baptism Record Albany Reformed Church, 1683-1804, 16 Aug. 1761: His baptismal record shows parents as Izak Valk and Marytje. Cornelia (this is obviously an error on the part of the transcriber, with the male name Cornelis being rendered as Cornelia). Sponsors Coenraad Hoogtelling and Cornelia Hoogtelling.

[60] Ontario Historical Society Papers & Records, Early Records of St. Marks and St. Andrews Churches, Niagara ON, (Vol. 3, 1901), Marriages 1795. Mar. 24. Cornelius Volick, br., and Eve Larraway, spinr.

[61] Transcribed and Indexed by Arthur C. M. Kelly, Baptism Record St. Paul's Lutheran Church 1728-1800, (1977), Schoharie Lutheran #680 Parents Isac Falk, Maria Child Annaje, bpt 26 June 1763. Wit. Matthes Werner jr, Eva Zahen.

[62] Transcribed and Indexed by Arthur C. M. Kelly, Baptism Record St. Paul's Lutheran Church 1728-1800, (1977), Schoharie Lutheran #810. Parents Isac Falk, Maria. Chid Sturm born 17 Feb 1765, bpt 19 Feb 1765 Wit Nehrich Werner, Catharina Zahen.

[63] Transcribed and Indexed by Arthur C. M. Kelly, Baptism Record St. Paul's Lutheran Church 1728-1800, (1977), Schoharie Lutheran #923. Parents Jost [sic] Falck, Maria. Child Sophia born 11 Apr. 1766 no bpt date. Wit Johannes Werner and wife.

[64] Transcribed and Indexed by Arthur C. M. Kelly, Baptism Record St. Paul's Lutheran Church 1728-1800, (1977), Schoharie Lutheran #1042. Parents Isac Falck, Maria. Child Elisabeth born Dec. 1767 no bpt date. Wit. Christopher Werner and wife.

[65] Transcribed and Indexed by Arthur C. M. Kelly, Baptism Record St. Paul's Lutheran Church 1728-1800, (1977), Schoharie Lutheran #1101. Parents Isac Falck, Maria. Child Catharina b. 25 June 1769 no bpt date. Wit. ____ Brath and wife.

[66] Upper Canada Sundries at National Archives (Rg5 A1 1796 p 127-138) The marriage certificate of Albert Hainer and Catharine Folluck d/o Isaac.

[67] Transcribed and Indexed by Arthur C. M. Kelly, Baptism Record St. Paul's Lutheran Church 1728-1800, (1977), Schoharie Lutheran #1223. Parents Isac Von Falckenburg and Maria. Child Jan born 25 July 1772 Beaverdam. no bpt date. Wit Jan Bradt and wife.